# JULIE KENZLER

## Hope Follows

### Reclaiming the joy that is yours

First edition

ISBN: 978-1-7360511-1-5

Cover art by Jack Kenzler

This book was professionally typeset on Reedsy.
Find out more at reedsy.com

*For my sister Tammy, who taught me how to laugh contagiously,
live adventurously, and love unconditionally. How I miss you.
For my husband Kurt and children Jack, Ryan, Maggie, and Evan,
who held my hand every part of the way in saying goodbye to
Tammy. You are my super heroes.*

# Contents

# Introduction

Welcome to my book. I'd like to think of us as friends, because we are sharing this book together as author and reader. We have one more thing in common besides being new friends: the experiences of ups and downs in life. Our unique journeys are filled with a variety of weather-like patterns like shade, sunshine, snow flurries, rain, and even devastating storms like hurricanes and tornados. Just as our struggles are different, the hope that comes afterwards is unique; it's more like a gift we unwrap.

Each of the chapters in this book will reveal a new layer of my "hope" discovery. I can't say I put on a miner's hat and got out my flashlight in search of hope. Though that sounds like an adventure I might enjoy, this was more of a discovery similar to finding a really unique rock on a trail. I love to hike, and when I see a rock that captures my eye, I'll toss it into my backpack.

\* \* \*

I was minding my own business walking through life and came face to face with moments of struggle, setback, and strife. God was so gracious to give me images and object lessons that revealed hope. Now, I have an enormous backpack of "hope" rocks, figuratively speaking. *Hope Follows* is a collection of the behind the scenes look at how I found new hope after a tragic loss. Grief was my new, unwanted house guest. Hope was shattered off my radar.

On November 10, 2013, my beautiful sister Tammy was raking the crunchy autumn-scented leaves in her yard. Knowing how much I missed my home state of Indiana in the fall, Tammy took good care of this younger sister in the deserts of Arizona. For years, she mailed boxes of leaves to me so I could see, touch, and smell the loaded reminder of my childhood in our wooded yard. But, this day was different for Tammy. She typically would see her dog of 17 years, Peanut, jumping around the leaves. Not today. Peanut had died a month prior. It was a daily battle of grief, depression, and hopelessness for Tammy.

As she continued raking more leaves, she just couldn't do it anymore. The images of Peanut running through the leaves haunted her mind. She told her husband that she needed to take a break. Tammy grabbed her Bible and suited up for a usual, tranquil ride on her motorcycle into the town's Starbucks. Tam loved her "five bucks" as she endearingly called it. Here's the part I can't even stand to share; Tammy didn't make it to the Starbucks. A drunk driver crossed the median and struck my beautiful and sweet sister. She struggled to hold on to her life and after two hospital admittances and an emergency helicopter flight to a trauma level hospital, my sister breathed her last breath. Hope. Nope. Not here. Not now. My brain and heart shouted, "NOT EVER!"

\* \* \*

iv

I miss Tammy to the deepest part of my whole being. She was more than a sister, but also a best friend and like a mom to me, a devoted aunt to my children. She loved her Lord deeply and her family and friends unconditionally. Her sincere, caring heart and incredibly contagious laugh I couldn't bear thinking was gone. I was devastated and walked for a long time without happiness, finding most of my days dreary and filled with tears - unsure if I would come out of that pit.

Living through trials and tribulations, ups and downs, tragedies and battles, our hope naturally becomes stifled and quite blurry. But, one day when you least expect it, something changes. Some may even notice the change that you can't see. Maybe you feel it but think it can't be real.

I remember the day that I recognized a glimpse of new hope; my son Evan and I were at home. It was about two years after losing Tammy, and I felt a feeling I hadn't experienced in a long time. I was full throttle with energy and joy. As I bounced around the house doing chores, Evan made a comment that is vivid in my mind as if it were yesterday. He said, "Mom, you have so much joy and seem so happy, like I have never seen before." Evan was right. I did feel a new level of something really good. What was this feeling, and where did it come from? I couldn't even explain it.

I began to further unravel these somewhat strange emotions that seemed as new as a Christmas morning present when I was a young child. It happened. The door of new hope had flung wide open. After two years of grief work, counseling, grief support classes, a library of grief books, Bible studies, prayers, journaling and blogging, I opened the door to new hope and joy. The deep pain and sorrow seemed to be on the route to healing, which meant there would be room for something new, something good.

Someone once told me that the depth in which you love a person who is no longer with you correlates to the depth of pain you will feel. Hence, my relationship with Tammy. When we lost her, I felt empty, having no hope of moving past that tragedy.

This book is my cry to you, my friend, that you can find hope in the storms of life. Losing Tammy was indeed a deep wound that I knew the only direction I could go would be up. I had to get out of the pit of grief and find hope somewhere. But, I didn't know how I would get there or how long it would take.

\* \* \*

Woven into many chapters you will find stories that include Tammy, because she is part of who I am today. For me to transform from a hurting woman into one who sees hope all around, I can't just sit around and bask in this celebration. When I first started blogging, I began to see inspirational and hope-filled messages in so many places that I couldn't contain it to just my journals.

The time to write a book, a dream I have had for 20 years, had arrived and was parked in my garage. I had the key, and I needed to turn the engine on. I finally had the content, though indeed NOT the content I originally had planned for my first book. I had other ideas for a first book. But, things changed, and the authorship process began.

Aren't you glad you won't have to wait until the last chapter to see how hope slowly and subtly returned to me, and how it can for you, too? No yearly membership fees here. No quick and easy surveys. Take your time. No deadlines. It's just you, your hurts and broken pieces. Imagine the possibilities of a hope-filled life in the face of sorrow, struggles, and hardships.

\* \* \*

After each chapter you will find a *Hope Follows* statement showing hope can follow any type of difficulty we face, little or big. Next, a carefully selected Bible verse is listed for added inspiration. Finally, I have crafted practical ways to live out this new hope and joy with a "Big Idea" suggestion that concludes each chapter.

I couldn't be more grateful and excited you have picked up this book to start your own journey of reclaiming your hope and joy. Are you ready? Let's get started.

\* \* \*

*Hope Follows. Hope Follows* the hard stuff;
and believe me, it works.

# Let the Pruning Begin

As we begin our journey of finding hope in the midst of life's hard moments, allow me to reflect on the word "glean". What do you think of when you hear that word? The first image I have is of the toothpaste brand "Gleem" from long ago. I bet you didn't know this 1950's toothpaste was later replaced with Crest Fresh and White in 2014. Enough with the trivia; let's dive into the word *glean.* Two definitions are found in the *Merriam -Webster Dictionary.*

1. To gather information or material bit by bit
2. To pick over in search of relevant material (*gleaning* old files for information)

Go with me on this *glean* trail. Glean can also mean to clean out piece by piece, little by little. Gleaning can be thought of as a careful, methodical practice. When we are stuck in a painful or hard moment in our lives, our hearts are crowded with worry, fear, and other negative emotions. If we glean out unfavorable feelings, won't we then create space for something more life-giving like new hope and joy?

Sometimes, I think we don't have space for hope and joy to replace our hardships and struggles, because we feel stuck. Stuck, like a kid playing in the mud when his shoes suddenly sink and disappear. To wear those shoes again, they have to be pulled out of the mud and cleaned off. This may sound elementary, but the concepts of cleaning, pruning, and transformation are huge when it comes to regaining hope and joy in our lives.

The first couple of years after losing Tammy were dark for me with the opposite of joy and laughter coming out of this lady. I felt stuck. My life was not in order and a little messy. More solemn than joy-filled, I was the center of worry around my home. I heard my children say, "What will happen to Mom? Will she be okay?" Their comments frightened me, as I saw the reality of their worries and fears. I knew change was a must in order to improve the atmosphere in my home, but I wasn't sure how this could happen.

The idea of cleaning and pruning really hit me like a bright light bulb one day while working in the yard with my son Jack. I like an orderly and tidy yard, but pruning can really scare me. My husband Kurt trims like he could win a major award for "most" branches pruned. Seeing the bare trees and bushes always made me feel sad, unsure if there would be beautiful flowers and leaves again. Guess what, Mr. Engineer Kurt was right. They did return to their vibrant colors.

As Jack and I were cleaning up the yard and cutting off the "old" parts of the bushes and trees, I knew there would be new growth one day as there always had been. What seemed like an eternity was really only a few weeks when I began to see life in the trimmed bushes. As I looked at the once pruned grapevines creeping up the patio pillars, I stood in awe and wonder. Looking deeper into the vines, I saw tiny green grapes, probably hundreds! Soon, we would be eating those juicy, yummy grapes.

When trees and plants are left without pruning, they become wild, messy, even appearing old and dull. Cleaning up the dried up grapevines allowed for more space to have new growth. Just like the plants and trees, we have times in our lives that are barren, dry, and even messy. Losing my father when I was in high school and then losing Tammy in our adult years, I was consumed with sadness and uncertainty.

As an adult dealing with grief, I could see the messy and unhealthy parts of my life that needed some pruning. I would never suggest that losing a loved one is a way to allow new growth. But, I will tell you that after loss hits, you can either stay grief-stricken or you can take steps towards gleaning and pruning the negative stuff to make room for the hope and joy that is yours.

Losing my sister was very different from losing my father. As adults, Tammy and I had shared so much of our lives together. I was devastated and walked for a long time without happiness, finding most of my days dreary and filled with tears. I was unsure if I would come out of that pit and felt like that pruned grapevine.

The Lord was so faithful to walk with me, holding my hand in the dry and weary desert of grief. The new growth of hope that I began to experience came in so many different forms. My hikes became more of a fun time to appreciate the mountains, instead of time to weep and throw rocks out of anger. Intentional lunch dates with friends became more frequent and a time to laugh and encourage one another in our lives. My marriage began to have less strain as I gave more time and attention to Kurt. I began to plan trips taking each of my children back to Indiana, sharing my childhood memories and favorite places. Seizing opportunities to create memories, just like Tammy and I always had, became a new passion of mine.

Coming out of a long stretch full of grief and sorrow, I began to see life with a whole new perspective. I felt like I had been pulled out of a swimming pool that I was wading in for years. I wasn't afraid for God to help prune out the bad feelings. The anticipation for how God would transform my life began to grow. I can't wait to share more with you as we discover new hope together.

\* \* \*

### *Hope Follows a time of pruning*

\* \* \*

*"I am the vine; you are the branches. If you remain in me and I in you, you will bear much fruit; apart from me you can do nothing."*
*John 15:5*

**Big Idea** - Write the word "HOPE" on a sticky note and put it on your bathroom mirror.

# Make a Memory

*A*s Mother's Day approached one year, I couldn't help but think of the movie "Guilt Trip" starring Barbra Streisand and Seth Rogen. One of my mom's favorite actresses was Streisand, who is such a talented actress and singer. The movie is filled with both hilarious and emotional moments. Streisand plays a widow whose son pays her a visit while on a work road trip. Despite the overbearing nature of his mom, Rogen decides to invite her along on the trip and plans to arrange an encounter with one of her former lovers. Mom and son find their week together a mix of crazy adventures, hurt feelings, and genuine love. There is nothing as beautiful as seeing a relationship rekindled.

As a mother, I can relate. In fact, as a daughter I can relate. Relationships are a puzzle of experiences and emotions that contribute to the people we become. The movie concludes with a sweet moment, and I will not spoil it for you. The cool lesson I took away from the story is to not be overly involved with my children, especially as they grow up to be adults. However, this is easier said than done.

In one scene of the movie, Streisand sits in the waiting room where her son Rogen has a work appointment. Laughing hysterically at how she licks her fingers to help fix his hair, I bet I'm capable of doing the same thing. One of the hardest jobs for a mother is to transition from the mom who is needed daily to the mom who is barely needed. Although I claim having the purest of intentions when I offer suggestions to my adult children, the reality is that they need me more as a friend and mentor. What our older children want and need is for mom to be present and genuinely interested in their lives.

One of my proudest achievements as a mother is the abundance of pictures I have taken over the decades. I never disappoint my family on trips and special occasions with my reputation for taking way too many pictures. Kurt and the children may have been over-the-top annoyed, but they will cherish looking through them in years to come and recalling the memories only a picture can spark. Isn't it cool how the power of pictures can take us back in time?

When I reflect back to when my children were little and building with Legos or playing with the doll house, I wonder if I spent enough time joining them. I did play often, but there were definitely times when I was more absorbed with household chores or other tasks.

I find myself on a virtual seesaw of ups and downs, where I battle myself as a parent. Was I a good mom when my children were younger? Did they each get plenty of play time with me? Was I a safe place for them as a struggling teenager? This is something I toil with that can send my mind and heart into a funnel cloud whirling around me.

I am learning more about enjoying each moment and making memories. A sweet neighbor friend came to my side throughout the first years after losing Tammy. Cynthia was so kind and knew my heart was broken. On Tammy's trips out to Arizona, she had gotten to know Cynthia. Several times Cynthia dropped off a little something and often sent me encouraging texts; I am forever grateful to her.

On one particular day, Cynthia brought over a pie, and we sat and talked. One further gift she gave to me was the concept of *making a memory*. Now, I know all about making memories through elaborate parties and unforgettable trips, but she was talking about everyday small memories that are invaluable and not costly. She encouraged me to find moments in each day that can be stored into our hearts. We talked about how sometimes we thought the bigger things were the special memories, but often it's the little things that become the bigger memories.

Tammy was all about doing the meaningful, smaller things to show love through a hand written letter, a phone call, or sending leaves in a box. As Cynthia and I cried and laughed together, she left me with a big hug and said, "Julie, we just made a memory!" Yes, we did!

What's a recent memory you made that is small and gives a sparkle to your heart? Be on the lookout; be watchful. I remember when Ryan was trained as a lifeguard for his first summer job. He stood at the pool with his eyes focused on the assigned area of the waters. I loved watching him. He stood bravely and confidently. I would have been so distracted, and I definitely would not have wanted to clean out you know what from the pool that was left by some child who couldn't make it to you know where, the bathroom.

Instead of keeping our eyes open for meaningful moments, we often spend time reflecting on our mistakes and missed opportunities. Just like a soothing ointment comforts the pain of a wound, making new memories helps to replace the things we feel we messed up with or lost time with. How about if we act like medicine to people in our lives and seize moments that create new memories filled with love and laughter?

With whom can you make a memory? Who can use some one-on-one time with you? How about surprising your adult child by dropping off their favorite lunch? Hang out with your child and hear about what they are doing in their lives. Yes, ask your teen child about the game they are playing and why they find it entertaining and challenging. Do you know a single mom who could use some help at home? Could you drop off flowers for her mom as a thoughtful surprise? How about an elderly neighbor who needs help cleaning up their yard? The ways to "make a memory" are endless. Just think of the joy and hope you can gift to someone with only a little bit of your effort and time.

\* \* \*

### Hope Follows lost time

\* \* \*

*"May your unfailing love be my comfort, according to your promise to your servant."*
   *Psalm 119:76*

**Big Idea** - Do something special for a friend or neighbor.

# A Special Number

I don't want to say it is an "aging" thing, but I do get numbers mixed up often. More specifically, I tend to get the year mixed up. Now, how hard is it to remember the year when you have 365 days to use it? Forget that I am a teacher who should have simple things like the year completely memorized; but oddly, I find this a challenging task. As 2016 approached, I kept calling it 2017 without any idea why. Even on a Facebook post I wrote, "Happy 2017!" Thankfully, my older son's sweet wife, Alexandra, spotted it for me! At that time, Alex was Jack's girlfriend; how wonderful she didn't let my odd antics keep her from marrying such an amazing man. They are a special couple.

There I was in 2016 writing 2017 on everything. I wrote it on my new message chalkboard in the kitchen and even on checks (remember those are the things that are paper – nobody knows that in an age of payment convenient apps!) Come to think of it, I wondered if I had a grudge against the number 16 as I was really persistent to ring in the year ending in 17.

There is something about that number that resonates with me.

Why does this happen? Why do we mix up our dates? I have reason to believe we may have too much on our minds. They are on full blown overload by the end of a year. Think about it, at the beginning of a new year, we have just topped off the past 12 months in one of the busiest times on the calendar. December is filled with festivities and traditions, lists and errands, projects and final exams.

I can best compare a busy month to that of swimming. My swimming pool is more like an oval or kidney bean shape. To get a good workout in, I need to do a ton of laps in my shorter pool. As I approach the other side of the pool, I really could take another breath, but why stop my momentum when I am inches from the wall! I can feel my body fighting, "I want air. Oh, you're almost there; just wait." This is how I feel during the month of December; I'm running around barely taking a moment to sit, relax, and BREATHE!

I'm thinking that due to all the spirited hustle and bustle at the end of the year, our minds are technically not ready for new digits. I continued to be puzzled by the meaning of 2017 and why I kept writing that number instead of 2016. It finally came to me!! Have you ever had a "special number or date"? The kind of number you say is your "favorite number" or "lucky number". A number that you see over and over throughout your life. The special number that creates a sense of calm inside for some odd reason. My number is definitely 17. Not 2017, but 17. I didn't even know that this number which once brought upon feelings of sadness and hopelessness would one day be a special number in my life.

On a cold winter day, in my sophomore year of high school, I used the classroom phone to call my mom and arrange a ride home after Spanish Club. During the phone conversation, there was an emergency break in the call. This was a feature before call waiting existed, and a real operator would create an emergency phone call interruption at the request of another caller. I telephoned back at my house and was told to please find a ride home right away. At age 16, I was trembling with worry as I rode in the car of my kind teacher.

Upon arriving to my house and walking through the door, my mother had me sit down on our couch. She shared the horrific news that my father had died in his sleep the night before. I recall jumping up and down in panic and falling into the couch with screams and tears. It was a horrible shock to my heart and mind.

The date: *January 17, 1985.* My dad had finished building our fourth home in the summer of 1984, and we settled into our new location quite nicely. However, my parents were facing some big challenges in their marriage and in the family, so he moved out to live with a friend around December. I hated that.

On the night of January 17th, my dad picked me up from my work at a theater and drove me home. He didn't let me drive when it was snowing, and there was a near blizzard that week, I recall. Late that night, we sat in the car in the driveway, and he told me I didn't need to be in the middle of what was happening between him and my mother. He reassured me that they both loved me very much. After a long hug and both of us in tears, he drove to where he was staying. How would I ever know that this would have been the last time I would see my dad alive.

The number 17 was a dreaded number to me after that day of losing my kind and loving, hard-working father, Jack Herbert Toellner. For many years afterwards on January 17, I would recall how my world was shocked with loss and forever changed. I hated that day and the date on the calendar.

I firmly believe God puts special people into our lives to help us connect with other people. One night on February 17, 1989, my dear friend Terri begged me to meet her and some friends at a happy hour. I was sad and disappointed over a break-up with a boyfriend but reluctantly agreed to go out. It was this night that I met my husband, Kurt! To think I would meet a Purdue graduate and fellow Hoosier in Arizona, and then marry him and have four little blessings we call Jack, Ryan, Maggie, Evan. That is utter craziness! God is forever sovereign and awesome as he plans out so much goodness and hope in the midst of unknowns and sadness.

Guess what day we got married?? Yep, you guessed it, on the 17th. October 17, 1992 was a beautiful fall day in Arizona we selected to exchange our sacred marriage vows. Each month on the 17th, I have a tender spot in my heart. I know that God turned those dark, terrifying years without my Dad into beauty, happiness, and a promising future.

Now, as I write this chapter I just realized a certain connection for the first time in 31 years. Remember, I was a *sophomore* in high school when I lost my dear father, leaving my heart broken. It was in my *sophomore* year of college that I met Kurt, the person whom God put into my life to complete me in holy matrimony. Oh, the HOPE finding moments you can put into your pockets when you look around and count your blessings.

I continue to miss my dad and remember the sad day on January 17, 1985, but it will not hold me hostage to gloom forever. Think about your own life and the times you have seen near coincidences. Here's a little nudge: maybe it is a message or gift from God. It may not seem like a big deal, but when your heart feels that joy and renewed hope inside, think again at the significance.

Maybe you have a special number, saying, or motto that you identify with. There is so much to say about symbolism; God gave us many word pictures in the Bible to teach valuable lessons. I love the promise that came with the colorful rainbow, to never flood the earth again. Then, there is the simple, no frills manger where Jesus was born. We see a symbol of the Savior's birth in a common place, nothing fancy and royal in earthly terms. This speaks loudly to me that God uses us just as we are. No special skills or certificates are needed to share God's love. Look around you to see the reminders of your life purpose and meaning; your story matters.

\* \* \*

### *Hope Follows heartbreak*

\* \* \*

*"Count it all joy, my brothers, when you meet trials of various kinds, for you know that the testing of your faith produces steadfastness. And let steadfastness have its full effect, that you may be perfect and complete, lacking in nothing" James 1:2-4*

**Big Idea** - Think of YOUR special number, and count the ways it makes you smile inside.

# Mommas

❧❧❧

*D*o you forget to complete assignments or projects, wake up late, lose things, or take too long to get out the door? Do you lose track of time being absorbed in a project and then totally miss some other commitment? Are you frazzled and late to appointments or thoughtfully 30 minutes early like my mom? Maybe you are a person who is timely (this is Kurt) or maybe late (more like me). We all have the same 24 hours in a day, using it in our different ways.

This makes me think about motherhood. Motherhood is kind of like that. Mothers all have 24 hours in a day to squeeze in every little task and activity. But, each mother's daily routine and path looks different. In fact, even though mothers share the same title as *Mom*, it is their unique motherhood role that defines them. Allow me to share some of the Mom roles I am familiar with.

A mother who becomes a widow is someone to be forever respected and honored. Kurt and I both lost our fathers at early ages, leaving our moms to a life of single motherhood. No matter how a mom becomes a single mother, Kurt and I have always carried a deep passion and burden to help widowed and single mothers in some meaningful way. Whether the gift comes in the form of a gift card or meal, flowers and a note, yard work assistance or car maintenance, we jump at the opportunity to help in some way. To Donna Jeanne, Kurt's adopted mother, and Marie, my mother, we salute you and have the upmost respect for your tenacity as a widowed, single mothers. These are hardworking, selfless women.

Sadly, another kind of mom is one who has lost a child. Oh, my heart aches for them. Shall we not be timid or scared to sit by their side with a hug and heart of generosity. One of the most amazing women whom I know that has lived through such devastating loss is my sweet mother-in-law and Kurt's biological mother, Patty. She lost two of her four children in their adult years. Mamoo, as her grandchildren call her, is a woman of love, grace, character, and strength. She has endured some tough and tragic losses, I know nobody else like her.

Another type of mother whom I know well is the step-mother. I don't have a step-mom, but my mom was one. She married my father and made a vow that included his two daughters. Even though Tammy and Tracey were defined as my half-sisters, my mother raised us together. The name stepmother does not have a beautiful ring to it, and we owe unfortunate credit to the hundreds of television shows and movies that have showcased step-mothers as cruel and evil. My mom wasn't perfect, and in the 1960's most divorced and step families did not have the kind of support available today. Strife in blended families was more common than today's amiable blended families. Looking back on my childhood, I recall how my mom dressed us girls up for Sunday church and made good meals. She hosted parties for our birthdays and made sure we visited our extended family regularly, especially our grandparents. Step-sisters or half-sisters were not titles we used in our family. We were sisters. Thanks, Mom, for making a home that fostered love and devotion between us.

A new type of motherhood I learned about, as I approached my golden 50 year mark, was when I became a mother-in-law to my son Jack's wife, Alexandra. Wow, this was a whole new role to learn. I received no instructions on how to raise a child when I left the hospital except how to cover up certain boy body parts when changing a diaper. I am sure glad the medical staff gave me those directions! Day one having Jack home from the hospital started off with us forgetting some important items. Kurt drove back that night, leaving me home alone for the first time with my new infant. And you know what, it went pretty well; I loved that moment.

Do you think I would get instructions on how to be an A+ mother-in-law? Nope. I didn't get those either. I adore Alex, and grateful that any hard learning moments as a mother-in-law are cancelled with grace and forgiveness. She is a treasure in my life, and I strive to be a supportive and loving mother-in-law.

Becoming an in-law was a whole new level of parenting. I wasn't Alex's parent, yet she married my son; I was his parent. But, he wasn't living at home anymore and starting his own family. Early on, navigating the role as mother-in-law was filled with some curves and hills. I missed Jack coming home anytime and hanging out with us. I discovered this was a form of grieving over *what was* and *is no more*.

Conflicting thoughts filled my mind, "I'm so happy for Jack and Alex. After all, I raised my children to live happy, responsible lives that honor God with their spouses. But, I am sad and miss having him home." I reconciled my tangled emotions through one simple fact: Jack and Alex were bought together by God and their momma's prayers. My heart grew with gratitude, and conflict was wiped out. Shifting my thoughts became critical to developing a peaceable relationship with my new second daughter.

Hope in this new season became evident when I began seeing how this beautiful new addition to the family not only blended well, but added so much richness to our family dynamics. When you embrace your new "extra" child and allow them to be part of your family, they may just make you the best guacamole dip ever! When Jack married Alex, our family grew in blessings, and my kitchen meals became more flavorful. Seriously! I rely on Alex to add the seasoning and spices to my dishes. Thank you, Alex for making me a mother-in-law.

Motherhood is an ancient calling on a woman's life that we should continue to honor. Mothers go through some really hard moments, and appreciation is one simple way to ensure they feel valued. To the many Mommas out there, in the midst of hardships and struggles, may you find hope in treasuring each moment. When you are in the car waiting for your daughter to finish that mascara application (for the fourth coat!) or for your little toddler to grab his Elmo backpack that is lost in his messy little room, just sit there and breathe deeply. Look at them and smile. What joy is wrapped up in that "person you call son or daughter", who also can skillfully and successfully frustrate the daylights out of you.

Maybe you are in a hard time of parenthood and feel hopeless. You might even feel like an inadequate failure. If you feel that way, I can relate. Although this chapter focuses on mothers, I acknowledge that dads share the same emotions and feelings. You're not alone if you feel this way. Here are two paths to consider:

1. Keep your chin up, pray, and find a mom who can encourage you with hope from her story of hard to happy. Find a mom who you can encourage and cheer on.
2. Feel sorry for yourself, complain, and stay alone. Don't share your struggles with anyone, because "raising a child takes a village" is a fable.

With all that is within me, I hope you choose the first path, even if it isn't easy. I have tried parenting both of those ways and have found more hope and opportunity for positive change on the first path. As Dori in *Finding Nemo* says, "Just keep swimming, just keep swimming," for moms, I say, "Just keep momming, just keep momming." Stay the course being that wonderful mom you are to your children.

A message for all the dads out there: I hope this chapter has enlightened you into the different "mom" roles as you contemplate the mothers in your life. You, too, have different roles depending on the dynamics of your life as a father. May you feel appreciated and valued in your families as you journey through your parenting years.

To children we see throughout our day, sprinkle joy and love with a smile. My mom is 77 years old and the biggest fan in the universe of children. When she sees a happy, smiling child, she waves and thanks them for their smile. We don't really know the extent a smile and friendly greeting can touch someone, but it's sure worth giving it a try.

\* \* \*

### *Hope Follows challenging roles*

\* \* \*

*". . . being **confident** of this, that he who began a good work in you will carry it on to completion until the day of Christ Jesus."*
Philippians 1:6

**Big Idea** - Tell a mom she is doing a great job. Tell a dad he is doing a great job.

# Start Again

*I* love music for the single reason of how it elicits emotions with its lyrics and melodies. "Start Again" is a song by Rob Simonsen & Faux Fix Ft. The song is from the movie *The Age of Adeline*. I went to see the movie after my daughter Maggie told me it won a spot on her favorite movies list. The movie was indeed a good one, and I did not escape it without tears. Actually, I cry in pretty much every movie. I even cried in the *The Lego Batman Movie*.

*The Age of Adeline* is a unique and remarkable story with incredible casting. Adeline has an accident involving a car and lightning storm action, which causes her to not age, ever! She starts her identity AGAIN about every 10 years.

I'm pretty sure I have had an identity crisis with my career and vocation more frequently than every 10 years. For as long as I can remember, whenever I watched a movie or television show and saw some fascinating role, I had a surge of self-discovery overtake my mind. I dreamed out loud, "Hey, that's what I want to do!"

With *The Love Boat* television show, I wanted to be a cruise director. With any John Grisham movie or novel, I wanted to be a lawyer. The job suggestions were endless: FBI Agent, actress, politician, flower shop owner, news reporter, Olympic ice skater, judge, and anchor of a news show, to name a few. I had a mini identity crisis each time but enjoyed the trip down imagination lane.

As a parent, I can't begin to count the number of times I wanted to "start again" after any less-than-proud parenting moments. Mostly, they happened out of frustration when my children didn't listen to me, neglected their homework, or repeatedly ran late for school. Or the times when my child could have avoided doing poorly on a quiz by studying the material instead of memorizing social media pictures on their phone.

In these moments and many others that overwhelm parents, we often respond with a diminished amount of patience. Anyone relate?! Like an out of body experience, sometimes. I think back at those moments and wonder, "Why did I say that? Maybe I was too harsh. I probably made a bigger deal out of something that was trite." Thank goodness for second chances, grace, and lots of hugs after those not so shining moments.

One thing I miss about Tammy is her advice. We often shared our troubles and offered encouragement and ideas to one another. I think of my sister constantly and the lessons in life I learned from her. Whenever I had a problem with one of my children, I called Tam. Good thing I had four kiddos, because the odds were that they all wouldn't be having troubles at the same time; surely, one or two would be sailing smoothly during other tumultuous times. Tammy always had the best advice, and later in the day I would find an email with a lengthy attachment of research she found for my "problem" and how the Bible suggests handling it. I treasure those emails. We laughed so hard, because Tammy didn't have children; she would joke "How do I know anything about parenting when I don't even have a kid!?"

Well, you know what? I listened to her advice, because she was always spot on!! Something about being an outsider looking in seemed to help. I learned from Tammy that I can always *start again* by just prioritizing one on one time with my children. Spend time with them instead of worrying about how to fix them. Yep, that is surely some good advice.

I don't want to stay stuck in my troubles like an old scratched album on a record player. I willingly admit my failure points and weaknesses. When I have made a mistake or hurt anyone, I try to be quick in admitting my wrongdoing, apologizing and starting again.

One time, I hurt Tammy's feelings so badly. I can't even believe I said what I did; thankfully, we worked through our differences without lasting wounds. We had to be real and open with one another. Honesty and trust in a relationship are crucial to helping one another work through hidden pain, the kind of pain we are trying to mask.

The act of forgiveness is something that has always come easily to me. I have had some very hard moments with my mother and brother over the years, and I just can't imagine holding a grudge so deeply that my heart would close to them. Kurt tells me most people would have written off their family after going through such tumultuous times. I can't do that with my family or friends; it's just not part of my make-up. However, there is one person with whom I immensely struggled to forgive.

Dealing with the drunk driver who hit my sister, I could hate him and resent anyone who drinks and drives. How dare he be found not guilty based on some technicality. I could wish harm to him. I was filled with fury at this man. To see him in the courtroom and hear the details of this crime, a crime that took my sister away violently. I know better, though. I know that forgiveness is as much for me as for him. God calls me to forgive, and so I had to work on that one. I didn't have a choice.

Forgiveness was one tiny step towards healing over the loss of my sister. Freedom from oppression in this way doesn't happen easily, but it takes a ton of bricks off of your chest. I think when forgiveness is given away and received authentically that healing and hope can move into the wounded heart easier. I didn't study Psychology, but it's a hunch I have.

I miss Tammy's advice. I miss the influence, wisdom and love from my oldest sister. I am learning to *start again* with finding joy and fun. I have learned to not be down on myself or someone else for making a mistake. Don't think something cannot be fixed, especially a relationship. God is the best *repair man* of any life issue or wrongdoing!

I always tell my children, "We don't expect perfection from you, just your best." Then, again, even when they don't do their best and mess up, I am ready to offer a second chance, a *redo* or *start again*. I am so grateful that people offer me grace when I make a mistake; how can I not reciprocate. Don't you think we can benefit from a regular dose of *start agains* in our daily routines? Seems like some pretty good vitamins for the heart and soul.

\* \* \*

### *Hope Follows restarts and second chances*

\* \* \*

*"Generous in love—God, give grace! Huge in mercy, wipe out my bad record. Scrub away my guilt, soak out my sins in your laundry."*
*Psalm 51:1*

**Big Idea** - Think of one struggle you are facing that keeps resurfacing. Press the *restart* button and start again with a new perspective. Sometimes, all we need is a mind shift.

# What Type of Flower am I?

I often am found talking to myself. In fact, my family calls me out on not just talking to myself, but also narrating my life. Here's a little sampling of what my family hears, "I'm going to clean the bathroom, and then work on my blog. Oh, actually, I should start laundry so it will be running while I do other things. Yep, that is a good use of my time. Oh, I need to remember to pay the Gap bill." If you are guilty of this timeless act, please let out a big "Yep, me, too!"

The whole act of talking to my own self became most noticeable when Jack was a senior in high school; he was home at lunchtime most days. We each worked on our own tasks, and Jack would say, "Mom, you sure like talking to yourself a lot." Personally, I believe if I am not arguing with myself, I don't think it can hurt to have a chat now and then.

Truthfully, I am an active thinker, and my mind is always in fast forward gear. While watering my flowers one day I thought to myself out loud, "I wonder if I were a flower, which type would be me." I typed into the Google search engine, "What flower am I"? To my delight, I found a "quiz" to see what type of flower I would be based on answering a few peculiar questions.

The answer: *camellia*. Really? All I could think of was Boy George's song with Culture Club, "Karma Camellion". As I looked at the interesting flower, it reminded me of a hibiscus flower, which is one of my favorite plants. The summary of this "flower personality" read, "The *camellia* is symbolic for excellence, and really, would you accept anything less? You are a natural born leader with tons of confidence. You are energetic, ambitious, and passionate and these traits guarantee that you will go far." Oh, I liked the sound of this. But, I really wanted to be a "rose", because that is my favorite flower. Maybe I will keep re-taking the test until I become a rose!

Speaking of roses, I wanted to name our daughter Maggie, Margaret Rose. Before Maggie was born, Tammy and I were really obsessed with the movie *Titanic,* but Kurt wouldn't allow our child to be named a character from that movie. He said it would be healthier to have some separation from *Titanic* for a little while. I agreed but pouted a bit. Actually, the true reason I wanted to name her Rose was because of my grandfather's amazing rose bushes back home in Indiana. With Margaret being my grandma's name, it was a perfect fit. I still couldn't convince him. I guess watching the movie at the theater five plus times and on video about another five or so caused concern for an obsession alert.

Our beautiful rosebud daughter was named Margaret Julia. Guess what the funniest thing is about the names and the movie; remember the name of my oldest child? Jack. Does "Jack, Jack, come back Jack" ring a bell? That is Rose calling for her lover in the depths of the frozen ocean water. To set the record straight, our son Jack is named after his grandpas; *Titanic* had not come out yet.

As I researched more flowers and their meanings, I began creating my own "flower personality" bouquet. I thought of my strengths and weaknesses and the kind of person I aspire to still become. I'll keep the *camellia* for its ambition and passion. To that I will add the *bird of paradise* for joy, the *tulip* and *rose* for declarations of love, the *sunflower* for loyalty, and the *statice* for remembrance and memories. Add some *blue and purple iris* for more faith and wisdom, along with the *snapdragon* for more graciousness and strength. Those traits described me pretty good.

Even beautiful bouquets of exquisite flowers wilt in time when the water is depleted. As I work to develop those traits above, there will be moments I'm not looking very wise or strong. I may even be spotted being lazy and not motivated. Then, I add a little water putting effort into just one area; positive change is bound to happen. When we humble ourselves through awareness and acceptance of our weaknesses and strengths, we can't help but illuminate hope among those around us. How relieving it is to see imperfect people not trying to hide their flaws. If you ask me, that is encouraging and inspiring.

We have a pillow in our bedroom that says, "I married Mr. Right, Mr. Always Right." Kurt may be right about 95 percent of the time in discussions and decisions, but I bask in that five percent when he is wrong! It's such a humbling time for him. But in all seriousness, I have no problem being wrong or admitting my mistakes. Kurt is getting better at it, too, which isn't easy for an engineer who really is right more often than not.

It is such a freeing feeling to accept our flawed lives and make changes for the better. I notice God likes to use regular, real people as examples of making mistakes or having flaws. There are tons of stories in the Bible on this cycle. It's actually quite a beautiful thing. I think of Moses who had a speech impediment but was asked by God to deliver a message. God provided a "buddy" to help him along and speak for Moses.

Then, there was Jonah who refused to deliver a message to some really immoral people. God chose Jonah to warn the people in a town called Ninevah to flee from their sinful ways to avoid harsh judgement. God wanted them to change their lives for the good; Jonah, on the other hand, didn't really want to help them out. He decided to hide on a boat like he was playing the game Hide and Seek. Quite possibly, Jonah may have been afraid to go to the city where terrible acts were being done to people. It does sound scary to me. Thankfully, he put aside his pride and fear, submitting to God's instructions; the result - lives were changed and saved.

We can't talk about flaws without mentioning Paul in the New Testament. Whoa, that was one bad dude. Not the "cool" kind of bad, but he was evil. His original name was Saul, and he killed Christians out of hatred. Once he was humbled and had a transformation in his heart, he turned his life completely around and became known as the most important person in the history of Christianity, second to Jesus Christ.

Our weaknesses and strengths are like a bouquet of flowers on a kitchen table. Different colors, sizes, and smells create an orchestra of beauty to brighten up a room. May we take time to understand ourselves and develop our strengths while working on fine tuning and polishing the weaknesses.

Maybe you aren't into flower types and arrangements, so try applying the same concept to a large planter of cacti plants.

With 1400 species of cacti, I am sure you'll find a nice variety. What in the world can we do when we face our weaknesses and turn them into strengths?

\* \* \*

### *Hope Follows our weaknesses and shortcomings*

\* \* \*

*"But he said to me, 'My grace is sufficient for you, for my power is made perfect in weakness.' Therefore I will boast all the more gladly about my weaknesses, so that Christ's power may rest on me." 2 Corinthians 12:9*

**Big Idea** - Surprise someone special with a fresh bouquet of flowers, maybe your daughter, grandma, aunt, or a neighbor. I promise it will brighten up their day!

# Navigating the Waves

❧

"School is out!" the children yelled, ready to conquer summer vacation. One favorite summer tradition has been our trips to California. We don't usually go until July when we are baked, sizzled, and overdone with the Arizona heat. One particular summer was going to be different. We all needed some rest and restoration ASAP. Two days after the children finished school, we were outta there! We drove straight to Encinitas, California. What else do *Zonies* do who are from the desert lands? Go to the beach in Southern Cal. If you are unsure what this nickname, *Zonie,* means, you probably find it quite peculiar. The people of California fondly refer to us Arizonans as *Zonies.* They probably have a love/hate relationship with us. You see, we get in their way, but we bring mucho dinero to their beach cities.

On that particular visit, the waves were massive. I crave the setting at the beach for the sounds of the waves, the smells of the salty air, and the warmth of the sun on my face. Our routine: I relax and read, go in the water here and there. My husband buries the kids in the sand and then sleeps. The children jump the waves, ride the boogie boards, and build humongous sand castle communities. The biggest task the children take on is a group project digging a 4 foot cave-like hole in the beach, with other children joining forces. They can stay there for hours using the most creative imaginations. I love the vacation life. I love the beach and the ocean and the memories we have made there over the years.

When the children played in the large waves, I did worry, as a momma. One time, Evan (youngest child and most daring), was going out pretty far into the water. He was with his siblings, but I still kept my eye on him. The waves were crashing intensely. I have this vivid picture, still, of his little arm waving at me every two minutes. Totally serious on this, Evan was knee high and tossed up an arm to wave. Then, he was waist deep, a hand wave; jumping up and down, a hand wave; a wave crashes over him, a tiny little hand wave. I could still picture that bouncing boy with arms in the air and smile full of joy. Although my stomach was tight when a wave crashed over and was hiding him, the incredible peace washed over me when I saw that little hand waving. It reminded me of how God is ever present when we vulnerably face the open waters of trials and struggles.

During times of grief, we will experience something that resembles a wave. Although I did experience crippling grief at the early age of 16 after losing my father to a heart attack, the waves of grief as an adult and losing my sweet sister were gut wrenching. As I write my blog and mention my grief and new hope, it still doesn't feel real when I write about losing Tammy. It stings, burns, and aches. It's maddening to lose a loved one and even more intense as a result of a terrible, yet avoidable, tragedy.

The concept of grief crashing in on people like ocean waves is such a vivid word picture to explain what a person experiences during this painful time of mourning. The waves of sadness, anger, or any intense and negative emotion come from nowhere and smash its cold and strong waters upon you. Your system becomes shocked.

As you take battle with that wave and cry, scream, and attempt to catch your breath, the large crashing water then goes back into the open ocean. You can stand up now and walk around, even frolic in the calm, soothing waters. These are the moments of hope, joy, laughter, and happiness. Constant back and forth wave-like emotions become all too familiar during times of loss.

What I found was that the huge waves came frequently for the longest time. Daily, hourly. Then, as I poured myself into grief counseling, support groups, journaling, reading, family and friends support, and God as my guide, the intensity of the pain, the time between waves began to stretch. I don't see how "time" does the healing. Time simply passes. *We* do the work to move into a state of healing. This grief path is different for every person, but for all who want to find healing and hope, some work will need to be done.

Early in my grief journaling, I wrote, "Later on, the pain and intensity will be less, and I will be stronger emotionally, mentally, physically." I wrote that down because I heard it in a *Grief Share*[1] program video. Did I believe it? Not really. I didn't even have the vision to see that this could be me down the road.

What I want you to know is that whatever grief you encounter in your life, it will not take you under and defeat you. It may feel like it. But, you fight for your life to endure it, to heal from it. I have never worked so hard on one experience in my whole life. I worked diligently for an Accounting degree at Arizona State University, but the grief work I fought and battled through after losing Tammy and then going through a grueling trial was a whole different playing field.

"Embracing every moment" is my motto that I learned in the ebbs and flows of the waves. I still mess up and get upset with my kiddos, or I fall asleep early as Kurt and I watch a movie or read a Bible devotion. I still get stressed over doing too much or over dumb things. But, I also don't clean my kitchen every night like I used to. I don't dust the house or clean up with an obsessive attitude. I have lunch with friends more often. I smile at people who seem unfriendly or angry. I ponder life more.

Mostly, I am a different person. I travel a different journey. But, I know that this isn't the end of the story. Living through a bad chapter does not dictate the rest of my life story. Tammy is so present in my life and in my loved ones around me. Thank goodness God is the strong one to carry us through such hard times. Each day I can see the intentionality inside of me sparkle again. It's puzzling to me that even in my grief, I have these intense feelings of elation, joy, and hope.

I can relate to this quote by Warren Wiersbe, "It is a remarkable thing that some of the most enthusiastic people you will meet are those who have been through intense suffering." Don't let your suffering take you under. Jump around with those waves, and use their force to carry you into experiencing something more.

\* \* \*

### *Hope Follows crashing waves of grief*

\* \* \*

*"Then young women will dance and be glad, young men and old as well. I will turn their mourning into gladness; I will give them comfort and joy instead of sorrow."* (Jeremiah 31:13)

**Big Idea** - Sit outside and listen to the song "Oceans" by Hillsong United.

# You Won't be the Same

One typical hot summer here in Arizona, we spent evenings at the baseball field watching Evan play in the local Little League All Star games. All Star season was a whole new ballgame compared to the regular season (pun intended, of course). Practices were daily and sometimes twice a day for three weeks; after pre-season prep, there were nightly games. People don't really understand how hot it is in Arizona in the summer. If you didn't get the punch line yet, I'll let you know we have triple digit temperatures in the summer from morning until, well the next morning.

Imagine the hardworking, dedicated boys in their uniforms playing baseball, and they never complained. Their character and bodies were put through many tests beyond imaginable for a 10 year old. I may have empathy when my children struggle and are tested, but there is no sympathy. With any struggle, there will be rewards; these are golden moments for development and growth. That sharp looking team went undefeated until the semi-finals, losing by one run. What those boys gained instead of a championship will go far into their adult years.

I am a huge baseball fan with roots back to my high school days attending Cubs games. I confess I ditched school like in *Ferris Bueller's Day Off*. I didn't have the fancy car Ferris' friend had or participate in a big parade airing on television, but I remember having the time of my life at the games.

Admittedly, I have signed Evan out of school back when he was younger so he could go to a Diamondbacks vs. Cardinals baseball game with Jack. Isn't that the funny part, I'm a Chicago Cubs fan, Jack and Evan are St. Louis Cardinals fans, and Ryan is an Arizona Diamondbacks fan. We like to keep things spicy around here. I'll do whatever it takes to build adventurous memories; because my kids are my kids, they're pretty much stuck having fun adventures.

Speaking of long-lasting memories, anytime our family found an opportunity to serve and volunteer in our community, we were all in. I would like to say we did this every month when the children were young, but it was typically a few times a year during the holiday or summer. Initially, we found ourselves feeling a little lost or awkward, unsure of what we were supposed to do during the outreach activity. As our children went through high school, Kurt and I encouraged them to each go on an overseas mission trip before going into college. You don't return home the same whether it is local or global; your heart changes with new perspective, compassion, and appreciation.

Before having children, I experienced my first mission trip. Traveling with a youth group to Mexico to build homes, we were way out of our comfort zone sleeping in tents and enduring very hot and humid weather with "earwig" bugs residing in our sleeping bags! On that trip I tried really hard to sleep with my mouth closed at all times. Because I was sleeping, I have no idea if I was successful.

Along our parenting journey, we have had many wonderful opportunities to care for and love on people here in our homeland and afar. I have had the privilege to do mission work with my children and our church in the Native American communities here in Arizona. We found other places to help out, like Feed My Starving Children and various foster organizations.

One of my favorite times serving locally was one summer when we took otter pops to a men's recovery shelter, which was also a soup kitchen to the homeless at lunchtime. We handed out the cold, tasty treats to people who were worn and tired. The smiles on the people's faces were invaluable. And to my delight, I saw Jack, who was a pre-teen, off to the side with Kurt talking to a man who seemed to be shy and off on his own. I could tell the love of God was being shared with this lonely man.

When an opportunity came up for a global mission trip to the Dominican Republic the summer after Jack graduated from high school, I had been through a grief support group for one full session and searching for some purpose. It still wasn't a full year since we lost Tammy. Grief was still so much a part of my days. But, I felt a tug on my heart and sensed it was God urging me to take this step and go global. I went along with Jack and the youth team, hoping I could help in some way.

The significance of going with Jack on that trip was that we had planned a trip to see Tammy and our family in Indiana that exact summer. Since we would never have that chance, I felt an authentic impulse inside to do something that would stretch me. I knew Jack was being stretched, and I dared to go along. Plus, I once read that giving back to people is a healthy step in grief recovery. This was my chance.

Advice by experienced global mission travelers: "Go to serve and love the native people of that land, yes, but also we are to go and care for the missionaries who live there, helping them in any way needed. Go and fully engage in the experience. Be Jesus, regardless of how out of my comfort zone it will feel. Then, share that experience with those back at home." I followed the advice and had a life changing experience. I truly fell in love with the people in the Dominican Republic, both the missionary leaders and the native people we served.

I vividly remember flying back to the United States after that trip in the summer of 2014. As I sat on the plane listening to my music, tears just rolled down my face. Such a relief that it was super late at night and most everyone was asleep. I couldn't contain myself. All the emotions of losing Tammy collided with that trip of a lifetime with people who had more needs and struggles than I could ever know. Some of the discomforts included:

- working along side new friends with limited understanding of their native language
- the sleepless nights in a cabin that had enormous spiders on the prowl outside.
- the cautiousness of eating new foods, taking cold showers, and riding on scary buses
- being thousands of air miles from my comfy home

Through blurry eyes, I wrote in my journal, "I don't want to be the same. I want to push forward through this grief and have joy, and to share this joy with others. I feel the hope, Lord, that I will have joy again…in the morning after such a terribly huge loss."

As we bid farewell to our new friends, a couple of ladies came to me and shared how I touched their lives with hope. I don't even know what I said or did. But, it doesn't matter, because sharing this mutual gift of HOPE was all that we needed, and a hug with tears. Thank you, Lord!

Some people say that serving others through volunteer opportunities isn't for everyone. It is out of their comfort zone, or they aren't confident and skilled enough. Okay, I acknowledge that. Did you ever ride on a huge roller coaster for the first time? Did you know all the mechanical work behind how that roller coaster would stay on the track as it climbed up and then plunged down, making a loop not once, but twice? In the back of your mind, you were probably pretty nervous, but you rode it anyway. What did you feel after you safely arrived back to start? Pretty fired up and ready to get in line again? Yep, me, too.

Imagine that same feeling after serving food at a homeless shelter, packing boxes for a food pantry, gathering toiletries for a women's safe home, or delivering boxes of collected diapers to a teen pregnancy home. You'll be wearing a smile on the outside of you as well as the inside. Your joy and hope will not be contained.

Each time I served, it didn't come easy. There were things to learn, protocols to follow, environments that were foreign to me (even those in my own city), and people I didn't know. In the hardest moments, especially in the Dominican Republic, I could have sulked and cried, or hidden by my bed. I'm glad I didn't do that the night a tarantula decided to sneak into the cabins. Nope, I mustered up enough courage to press on. I saw hope in people's eyes that we served, so who am I to quit and roll over? My daily hardships were nothing compared to those who have less, are left out, or are lost.

An abundance of serving opportunities come up during the Thanksgiving and Christmas season every year, but why do we wait to help those in need only during those times? Let's search for experiences that allow us to volunteer during the summer and any time of year. I'm super excited about a new tradition for our family. We'll be taking turns finding outreach opportunities in each of our birthday months. What a tremendous joy to share the gift of time, kindness, and care with others, as a family.

\* \* \*

### *Hope Follows serving others*

\* \* \*

*"Serve wholeheartedly, as if you were serving the Lord, not people ... " Ephesians 6:7*

**Big Idea** - Brainstorm with family or friends a list of places to volunteer, and enjoy serving in your community together.

# Take Back Your Summer

$S$ometimes I think of parenting during the school year in terms of seasons. Summer is all fun while keeping the brain active. Fall is a time to get organized, and winter is consumed with lists and holiday festivities. Spring is a time to wind down, but you're trying to keep your head above the water with the numerous end of year activities. Summer is vacation time and party season; I'm a partier by nature. I'm pretty sure you would agree that summers are the favorite. I treated summers as a mom with an ETE approach: *exploring, travelling, and experiencing.*

Our usual activities when the children were young included Vacation Bible School, arts and crafts at home, playing in the kiddie pool in the backyard, driving Hot Wheels cars through a pile of shaving cream on the toddler table, Kids Summer Movie Pass, cartoons, and reading programs with the library. One of my favorite summer activities was Maggie's hairstyling salon. She had limited services to include hairstyles and head massages; haircuts were not services requested too often, so that was not on the menu.

As the children grew up, our summers changed a bit but still were filled with a whole lot of fun. Here's a list: beach trips, summer baseball, trying to get my kids to read, church youth camp, the children and I volunteering at Vacation Bible School, late nights, pool parties (we moved to a house with a full size pool), sleepovers, encouraging my kids to read, moody people when it hit 110 degrees, movie marathons, laughter and family meetings about reading more, urging my kids to read and keep a smart brain for the summer, hanging out with friends, me reading to them (yep, I gave up getting them to read), summer jobs, internships and mission trips.

Great experiences these were (speech influence from Yoda of *Star Wars*), and I couldn't be more content and grateful for the plethora of memories and photographs we have stored. Do you ever reflect on the summers of your own past?

When I think of my summers growing up, I have great memories of riding bikes to our local pool and buying my favorite ice cream bar at the snack shack every day (*I still buy it when on those rare days I see an ice cream truck - the strawberry crunch bar!*). My friends and I camped in a tent in the backyard. My sisters and I swam in the lake behind our house. We stayed overnight at our grandparents' home and played with cousins. The attic in our grandparents list barn was the setting for a lot of imaginary playtime. With our aunts' prom dresses and furnishings, we played house like we lived in the *Little House on the Prairie* days.

A favorite childhood summer memory was building our homes with my dad. Curiously, he built a new home every few years, and it happened to be in the summers. Helping Dad kept us out of trouble, for at least those summers anyway. I've been told that my dad would get bored with the current house he just built and have some great ideas for a new house. Thus, the plans would be drawn. He was so talented. One move was literally four houses down; it was a larger lot for our three-wheelin' fun with a tire swing in the woods. I'd say it was worth it.

Thanks, Dad, for those timeless home building lessons AND the White Castle burgers for our lunch breaks!! The greatest part of moving into one of the new houses was the fresh carpet. Dad let us pick out our carpet color, and I think I picked pink one time. Before moving all our furniture and belongings into the house, we slept on the carpet for one night. Ahh, the smells of new carpet today at Home Depot put me back in time to those endearing days.

Wait a minute! Have you ever wondered why adults no longer have those carefree childhood "summer times" anymore?! How did this happen? Who was in charge of this crazy idea? Was there a vote? As a working parent, there really aren't any breaks. If I want a day off I have to go on a mission trip or to the local spa and pay $40 for a day to sit by the pool reading a book and eating their delicious trail mix.

Oh, my spa days. How I love the smells, the relaxing music, the "chill" environment with everyone walking around in their white robes and lying around on lounge chairs. If you haven't done this ever, I dare you to try it out. Men and women! Take a journal, magazine, or book. I promise that you will feel refreshed. Kurt's favorite type of "chill" day is *riding* his dirt bike or in the garage working *on* the dirt bike. He loves the smell of the desert air with swirling dirt and the sounds with the throttle wide open.

Recently, I wanted to see what it was like to be carefree again.

This may sound a little odd, but my idea of carefree was signing up for a college course. I don't have many hobbies besides journaling and hiking, and I wanted to try something new as I entered my 50's. Well, I decided to register with HarvardX for an online course called *Rhetoric and Public Speaking*. Attending Harvard Law School had been a dream of mine when I was young, and this fueled my idea to do something with Harvard.

What a blast to revisit even a tiny portion of a childhood dream not fulfilled. I loved the college experience of academics while attending Arizona State University for my Bachelor Degree in Accountancy. In my 50's, stretching my brain to learn new concepts and study the speeches of great orators like Martin Luther King, Jr., Charleton Heston, and Ronald Reagan became a new passion.

Kurt has always been a talented artist, and he recently took up coloring again. His coloring is in the form of designing t-shirts from the 80's, like "867-5309" and a U2 album cover. What a great way to recapture those moments from the youthful years and summer times. He even bought quality shirts and new art supplies. Watch out, because you may see his designs becoming popular one day. The headline, "Man in mid-50's Tired of Adulting, Makes a Fortune on Hobby of T-Shirt Designs". I believe in you, Kurt!

Don't let age stop you from embracing life in a more adventurous way. Whatever age you see on your driver license, I'm pretty sure you qualify to do most any hobby you once held dear to your heart. Don't doubt and feel hopeless to entertain ideas you have had for a long time. Dig into the trenches and rediscover your former hobbies and passions.

Find some "summer time" fun that works for you, regardless of what month the calendar is showing. Don't wait for June.

Go ahead, take back your summer love now! Revive the youthfulness inside of you.

\* \* \*

### *Hope Follows forgotten passions*

\* \* \*

*"Don't let anyone look down on you because you are young, but set an example for the believers in speech, in conduct, in love, in faith and in purity."* 1 Timothy 4:12

**Big Idea** - Make a list of hobbies or activities you enjoyed doing in the summers of your childhood. Is there one that you have interest in getting reacquainted with?

# Lonely Moments in the Kitchen

*B*eing a "Northwest Indiana & Chicagoland" native, I have a deeply rooted love for the Windy City. Falling in love with the sunshine of Arizona on a spring break, I decided to make the move to Tempe, to attend Arizona State in 1987. I regularly traveled back home to visit family and friends and couldn't wait to see views of the city from the airplane. Of course, as the years went by my post-college life grew busy with working, getting married, changing careers, starting a family with a dog and then children. Family Manager was my new title, and that is when I REALLY started working (without paid sick leave or vacation days).

This concept of twenty-four hour employment really hit me recently when I asked Kurt to help out more with meals. I had grown bored and frustrated, losing interest and creativity in the kitchen. "What is wrong with me?" I anxiously thought, feeling hopeless. He casually replied, "The meals are your department."

Whoa! I know exactly what you are thinking. Hold onto that thought for a few seconds. Before we get down on Kurt for this "oops" comment, I must say that he is a hard worker. My dad was a hard worker and provider for our family, and it is no surprise that I married a man dedicated to finding meaningful work that provides a quality, safe life for his family.

Kurt helps out around the house, with the children, and makes great pancakes. But, meals, I know it's a main role of mine as a mom who stays home and works part time. Get this, the other day I counted five times I was in the kitchen for extended time periods preparing meals and cleaning, all before dinnertime. I was tired of being in there! I do have kids who can help, but they were probably busy doing homework or more likely messing around. Still, I felt it would be enjoyable to have my husband, my partner in this adventure called life, bonding in the kitchen with me.

That was it!!! I WAS LONELY!! I was tired of being in the kitchen BY MYSELF while everyone else was out and about throughout the house. All I wanted was a little bit of company, someone to converse with besides my dog Ellie, who is committed to being in the kitchen 24/7. She is pretty great at cleaning the floor.

Once Kurt was alerted to my kitchen loneliness, he quickly apologized and came to work alongside me in making a meal. It was a blast to have him there! You see, I turned that hopeless feeling around and communicated a need. They don't call me a Communications Teacher for no reason. Reflecting back to Kurt's comment, I could have been offended, but pressed on to help him understand my feelings. More like I had a temper tantrum.

It helped for me to express myself, and now Kurt is in charge of Sunday evening dinners and cleaning up the kitchen when I make the other meals. Being the food and menu manager of our home is a privilege and an honor to serve and take care of my family. I totally don't feel ungrateful and whiny. I simply needed a little reprieve.

Our kitchen area doesn't allow for me to having viewing access to the television. One day a year on Thanksgiving, I love to watch the Macy's Thanksgiving Day Parade. I have a dream to visit some year, witnessing the artwork and talent first hand. For hours on Thanksgiving morning, I am in the kitchen preparing, cooking, baking, cleaning, and repeat. Because I kept running back and forth from the kitchen to the family room watching the parade, I know it took me much longer for my meal prep activities. "Can't somebody please help me, so I can watch the parade?" I cried out.

Communication. Communicating our thoughts, feelings, needs, and hopes are critical. Guess what, if we are prompt to share our needs or concerns, then we wouldn't get boiled up inside balking out S.O.S. rescue commands. Sharing the need should come packaged with details on what we are asking for and the reason. Problem solving can take place, and everyone will live happily ever after. Well, except in some Disney movies, so don't eat the apple from the basket or drop that glass slipper on the stairs.

When your need is met, the next time someone shares a need with you, you'll be more empathetic and ready to listen and offer help. That is cooperation, and I can picture Big Bird and Bob of Sesame Street singing a tune about it now.

Talking about cooperation and reciprocation, I may want to march on outside to hang out with Kurt in the garage when he works on his dirt bikes to offer some help and see how he's doing. But when I think further, he probably will not want me there. I talk too much. Isn't that funny how different we are?!

I know all he will want are some cookies and cold lemonade. And that is what I will do ... wow, there I go back to the kitchen (but, I like being in the kitchen to bake sweets!). What a funny turn of events!

With the people we love and with whom we *do life*, let us embrace our differences, our needs, and our desires. Let us serve and appreciate one another without hesitation.

\* \* \*

### Hope Follows loneliness

\* \* \*

*"Do nothing out of selfish ambition or vain conceit. Rather, in humility, value others above yourselves." Philippians 4:13*

**Big Idea** - With your family, create a weekend menu. Go shopping and prepare a meal together. Bon appétit!

# Healing Visit – Back Home in Indiana

*I* had no idea of the intensity with facing my grief and working through it. Grief is one of those things, like a snowflake, that no two people handle the same way. Nobody should evaluate and critique others for how they deal with grief. The large amount of work I put into grief counseling included support groups and homework for the group, various grief recovery books, writing to fill up numerous journals, weeping and shaking. Decision making seemed excruciating when using my foggy brain.

Over the first two years of grief work, I stretched and grew as a person. The positive experiences that began to pour in were abundant. The HOPE that followed the *tragic loss* of my sweet sister Tammy included a deeper walk with God; closer family relationships; comforting hugs that speak "you mean the world to me"; more quiet moments to sit and reflect; keen awareness of the world around me; intentional silliness and humor; new adventures and trips; quality time with friends; heightened awareness and acceptance of others; and a fresh, clear perspective of the most important things in life.

I developed a renewed commitment for my own health and wellness, a greater insight for what God called me to do with my grief and passion for sharing "hope" with others. I began seeing my life statement as "seize the moments". I read in a grief book that when you become a survivor of grief, you develop stronger character. Yes, I survived the tragic loss of losing my sister to a drunk driver, meaning I didn't give up on life. What truly surprised me was how God made beauty out of ashes, and I was a living example. I honestly didn't know how I would survive after that shocking day. But today, yes, I am living life to its fullest. Several emotions are capable of residing in me at the same time: joy, hope, and sorrow.

Travel and vacations have more meaning to me now. When we travel as a family, I have an itinerary. When family visits us in Arizona, I have an itinerary. When I visited Tammy with the children, she had an itinerary. See the trend. We were notorious for having an agenda to pack in EVERYTHING we possibly could in our time together on the trips. A plan and schedule was thoughtfully designed, carefully crafted, and beautifully executed to have the time of our lives. Don't get me wrong, it wasn't like being in boot camp; but having a rough plan worked to have an idea of the fun that awaited.

Not everyone values a packed agenda like Tam and I did. Kurt and the children do not like how I plan our trips. It's just how I am though, my sisters and I just pack things in and we are so good at getting things done! Maybe your family is like mine where they dread the plans or ideas for a trip or event, complaining all the way; but, after the experience, they can't stop talking about all the fun and hilarious moments. One would think I should have given up long ago at planning fun activities for my family, but I can't stop. I crave fun! I crave memories! Maybe I even enjoy saying, "I told you so!" to my crew who isn't so open to new adventures. No worries, because they are coming around.

Now, my children laugh at me and say I am to blame at how "close" they are today and probably won't be able to move far from each other. They say it is because I always had them do things together, like trips and activities. It was our family belief that you support your siblings at their games, recitals, and competitions. You know something; I'll take full blame for this one. Upon writing *Hope Follows*, my children's ages are 17, 20, 22, and 25. It's pretty cool to have my children super close at these ages. Tip: do lots of fun things and take lots of pictures, even when your family is getting annoyed. They love looking at the pictures and hilarious home movies now.

On a fall break one year, I took Evan with me on a trip back to Indiana. For all my trips back home, I had typically visited Tammy, who was a few hours south of our hometown. Remember, her huge checklist of what we will be doing? This time, with a mix of emotions, it was up to me to run the show and plan out our days, including fun activities mixed with nostalgia. I knew this was part of my healing process in the grief of losing Tammy, getting back to see our childhood homes.

I just needed to be in my hometown. I needed to be there in that beautiful Chicago town. I desperately longed to reconnect with my extended family and have some time with friends, too. How I loved sharing my life in Indiana with Evan.

To reminisce on good memories is like soothing balm to a wound.

Evan and I had a total blast. We did so much on our visit. Even though I hoped to swim in Lake Michigan (which we didn't), we still got to see it and run through the sandy beach with the wind hitting our faces. It was so cold, we felt like were going to freeze. It is in the unplanned moments that you remember most.

What a blessed and memorable time I had with Evan. We have so many memories to treasure and personal jokes to laugh about for years. He was so interested in everything I shared with him (when he wasn't playing on the iPad driving through the long stretches of open fields in Indiana). It was hard to be there without Tammy, but really, she is with me and in my heart always. Nothing and nobody can take that away.

\* \* \*

**Hope Follows cherished memories we miss**

\* \* \*

*"And my God will supply every need of yours according to his riches in glory in Christ Jesus." Philippians 4:19*

**Big Idea** - Take a moment to reminisce on your childhood by calling a cousin, aunt, or uncle you haven't spoken to in a while. Enjoy the chat!

# Don't Judge a Dog by its Look

*A*h, the weather is so delightful in the wintertime in Arizona. How I love the winters where we actually have cooler mornings and evenings to wear sweaters and scarves. During the day, though, the layers are peeled off to our warm weather clothing. Of course, it is always a matter of months before we hit the 24 hour, 100 degree mark. But every chance I get, I go to a park or the mountain for a walk or a hike.

On one particular crisp and cool evening, I took our dog Ellie for a walk at a nearby park where Evan was having baseball practice. I love this park for its great views of the mountain range and the treasured memories of my sons' baseball activities for 15 plus years.

On the flip side, I had a pet peeve at parks. When I walked Ellie on the park path, I grew quite nervous when I saw dogs off leashes. I understand some dogs are nice and well trained, but to be very honest, mine was NOT! Oh, she was sweet and nice with us, but Ellie in her prime years was a bit aggressive when she saw other doggies. But, on that one night at the baseball fields, we faced two huge dogs that were incredibly intimidating. Yes, the double "I".

Their owner was an older gentleman who did have the two dogs on a leash. From a distance the dogs appeared to be, well, LION CUBS! They were beautiful but looked very ferocious. Their fur was so thick and multi-colored, and at the same time they were big and scary looking. Handling Ellie with one lion cub dog was fine but two identical twins!? Before I saw the leashes connected to these supposed "wild animals", I said in my mind, "Those dogs had better be on leashes. Wow, those dogs look very scary. I should probably just turn around and run from those dogs. What if they attack Ellie or me and nobody knows?" Those were my crazy thoughts, completely and utterly irrational.

Guess WHAT!!?? As I approached and passed by the trio (two dogs + owner), clinching Ellie's leash, it was as if I went into a slow motion movie scene. Everything slowed down, my steps, my mind, and all that was around me. I could even hear Lindsay Wagner, The Bionic Woman, running by in that clicking sound. To my surprise, what I thought were lion cub twins were mellow, happy, and content dogs I had ever seen. They moved gracefully and slowly across the path before me; I wanted to reach out and touch them.

I WAS SO WRONG about those precious animals. They did nothing wrong to me or to my dog, and from a distance, I assumed they were vicious just by their appearance.

I totally judged those dogs, just as I have done with other dogs and owners. I often walked on edge with Ellie when in the company of other dogs. My nerves were always a pile of tumbleweed sticks as I wondered how the interaction would

55

go between our squeaky Border Terrier and any other breed.

What a good lesson that experience became as I learn and strive to not pre-judge people and to work on my own prejudices. Simple acts such as having an open mind and heart could lead to some pretty neat interactions with people who are different from us. One thing I noticed in my days of grief was the moments of heightened happiness in the form of a friendly hello to a stranger. It's as if I felt my duty was to be sure they have had one positive encounter in their day. I can hear my sister Tammy now from our many phone calls talking to a store clerk on the other end; she always had such a joyful, fun, and enthusiastic way with anyone she came in contact with.

Everyone deals with struggles, stress, and super rough times. When we come in contact with people who are different than us or whom we hold prejudices about, think about what kind of struggle they might be facing. Who cares what skin color or age they are or where they might live; we are basically all the same inside. We all face these challenges, so what makes me think I could be better than that person?

What made me think those big dogs were inferior to my dog? Why did I think those dogs were going to hurt my dog just because of their size? I was judging them; and it wasn't right. It isn't right to judge anyone different than myself. Taking it a step further, I shouldn't even be judging my own family members. But, guess what, I do. I do judge even those I am closest with.

That teachable moment in the park with the two lion cubs brought me a reminder for not getting lazy with how I view people. I intend to carry myself in ways that are approachable and kind to all those I come in contact with. There is no profit in prejudice. Having my own ideas and opinions with little or no knowledge sets me up on a throne. Jesus sits at the throne with God in Heaven, so I better keep my feet on the ground and sit in my rocking chair. Consider what we can be doing with our words and attitude instead of pointing fingers.

Could I somehow be the cause to brighten someone's day? Could I potentially lift someone's spirits who has been struggling with eviction notices? Or what about the person who just walked in front of me at the store line? Should I be unfriendly and rude because of the negative disposition they carry?

If I pause now and then to get fresh perspective, I could maintain a kind-hearted disposition even to someone who isn't treating me well. What if my smile causes them to lighten up a bit inside, and they go home to children who are misbehaving? Would they possibly recall a friendly encounter earlier that day and then take a deep breath before responding harshly?

Check this out! We can actually be an influence to creating a positive environment in homes we may never set foot in. You have that power in you. Just push those judging thoughts aside. They don't have any room in your mind. Put up a NO VACANCY sign.

Turn up the dial of friendliness, and dare to leave a positive mark on a random person. I decided to let God's healing balm soothe my wounded heart through giving away smiles and genuine compliments. I admit that I mess up at times and let out my frustrated, angry voice. One time, I was so annoyed with a driver on the road who cut me off unnecessarily, that I drove right up to the back of their car at a traffic light. I laughed and spoke to them like they could hear me, "Seriously, dude?! That was so ridiculous, and you saved no time doing that!" I kind of forgot about my smile and joy in that moment.

Thankfully, I can always have another chance.  Each day we have many chances to get it right.


\* \* \*


### *Hope Follows preconceived feelings and prejudice*

\* \* \*


*".... as the time when the Jews got relief from their enemies, and as the month when their sorrow was turned into joy and their mourning into a day of celebration." Esther 9:22*

**Big Idea** - For one full day, smile at everyone you encounter. Have fun with it!

# No More Should Haves

*D*o you have those moments when you see the most beautiful sun rays shining so triumphantly from the sky to the ground, through all sorts of cloud formations and blue hues in the sky, and stand in awe? I love when my children were young and shouted out, "Mom, it looks like Jesus up there! Oh, that cloud looks like a dog! And that one looks like a dinosaur!" The world of imagination is precious.

How I love the gifts of God's artwork in the sky and a child's tender, simple heart. In those moments, any emotion I may be feeling is on hold as I stand in wonder and astonishment, taking the sights in. In the early days of losing Tammy, those moments were medicine to my soul. I didn't know that more heartache was around the corner with a need for more times to be still.

Exactly two years and three months after losing my sweet sister Tammy, we lost Tom, her husband, on February 10, 2016. Tom took his life. I can hardly write this and look at the words without thinking this couldn't have been true.

After the raging battle of losing Tammy as a result of a drunk driver and during the shocking "not guilty" verdict at the final court hearing, our family had so many questions. But, it wasn't the final chapter. We were devastated all over again: Tammy, trial loss, Tom. I never doubted God walking with me every minute over those first years. I held onto God's arm like a child in a dark, unfamiliar place.

Where in the world do you find more hope after this? One place I found it was in learning that the "should haves" and "would haves" only create more complications with our emotions and heads.

I wrestled with those daunting thoughts many times: "I wished I would have called more, visited more, and reached out more. Did I do enough? Did I send enough pictures? Did I tell them I appreciated them? Why didn't Jack and I visit Tammy and Tom before his senior year in high school like we talked about? What if I would have done this or that? Could I have prevented anything? I should have called Tammy on that Sunday to talk, and maybe she wouldn't have left the house on her motorcycle." Questions like these will torment your mind. They did for me in the beginning of losing Tammy, just as they did in 1985, when my dad died.

How did I cope with those negative thoughts? Many people told me "Don't go there. Stop having those thoughts. You did all you could do. You loved them all you could." Honestly, although people meant well, telling me not to say those things didn't really help. I needed concrete, practical ways to counter the thoughts. Through the Grief Share support group, I started to learn some helpful principles and strategies, but I also came up with my own "coping skills" for those bothersome and unproductive thoughts.

When a "would have" or "should have" came to my mind, I sat on it for a bit. I recognized the sad moment and allowed myself time to reflect. Slowly, I began to realize those thoughts could only invade my mind if I allowed them. I had to face the thoughts head on. I couldn't stuff them down, as my mind doesn't work that way. I had to pivot my thoughts to something more positive.

That is when I began to shift my thinking to a special time together, a fun memory, or a tender moment. I looked through pictures and reminisced on the blast we had from a particular visit or trip. In pictures, I saw so much joy and laughter. When I first began practicing the switch from "should haves" to "what I DIDs", I recalled ways I stayed in touch through long phone chats and encouraging letters.

Probably one of the most helpful moments with overcoming regret was when Kurt told me that I did give much to Tammy and Tom. I shared my life and my children with them. OH, I loved doing that. I welcomed them and all our family as royalty into our home anytime they made the westward trip from Indiana.

Another time I can recall when "should haves" try to shadow over me is a trip to the Painted Desert with Tammy and Tom. They loved that area, and Kurt and I had never been. We met them at the beautiful site in northern Arizona and went on a big hike. Really, we climbed rocky mountains with no trace of a trail. We were the trailblazers! I still can't believe what we climbed with little children and a tiny barking dog. The movies from that day are worth more than all the gold in the world.

One time, Tammy fought me on Kurt and I giving up our bedroom for them. I wanted them to have a bigger room with their own bathroom. They left after a few days to ride their motorcycles up to the Grand Canyon. Upon their return, Tam bought us a rather nice gift card to a lovely hotel in Flagstaff. She appreciated the gesture of us giving up our room so much that she wanted Kurt and I to go on a nice getaway. I couldn't win with her! She always had the last "blessing" and fully enjoyed one-upping me.

More memories would flood into my heart as I worked to eradicate the "should haves" and "would haves". At least three times we drove our Honda Odyssey minivan 1500 miles over the prairies, through the storms, and into Hoosier Land we arrived. Staying at Tam and Tom's with our campfires and late night talks was one of our favorite traditions. Despite the complexity of driving across the country with multiple young children, seeing our family and friends was always worth the time, money, and effort. I have no regrets, only memories of fun times, endless car games, and a million potty breaks. Those are the things I focus on when I start to hear the whispering words, "You should have. Why didn't you?"

You can bet that changing my thinking took a lot of concentrated practice just like any new sport or hobby. Golfing is not my sport, but living in Arizona is a great place for the sport with its beautiful golf courses. When I have golfed, I thoroughly enjoyed driving the golf cart. One time, I took Ryan out to golf when he was in second grade. We got stuck on a bridge I later discovered was not meant for a golf cart. Why have the bridge, then?

I began running around the course calling for help. Then, I went back and sat with my embarrassed, smart boy, who points out that the cart can go in reverse. Yep, that's all it took! We laughed hysterically about that crazy outing, and I don't think he will go again with me.

Should I one day want to become a better golfer, I would need to spend some time practicing the swing and other skills. I know how to play baseball and make a good bunt, but swinging a golf club is totally different!

Learning to play golf will take PRACTICE to get my swing right. Practice makes permanent, not practice makes perfect. I like that. How about you? What do you do when you start thinking about all the "should haves" in your life? Don't let them torment you. Those stinkin' thoughts have no right to make you feel bad about what you did or didn't do with a special person in your life. Work through the thoughts as you pivot to special memories that bring a ton of joy to your heart. This is where you will find hope.

For always I will love you, Tammy and Tom, and for always I will miss you. I mentioned that our Tom passed away on February 10th, and this is a reading from that day on a devotional flip calendar titled, "Prayers of Hope".

*"Lord, free me from the need for answers. Help me to surrender. Jesus, you are the Good Shepherd. In Your Name alone do I find everything I need and all that I long for! You hold the keys of life, and the purpose of Your heart prevails. Creator of All - You have it all figured out. Jesus, forgive me for trying to take on what only You can handle. Be my focus. You are my answer. Amen."*

\* \* \*

**Hope Follows the should haves that steal joy**

\* \* \*

*"Finally, brothers and sisters, whatever is true, whatever is noble, whatever is right, whatever is pure, whatever is lovely, whatever is admirable - if anything is excellent or praiseworthy - think about such things." Philippians 4:8*

**Big Idea** - Tell yourself it's okay that you missed an opportunity to spend time with a loved one in the past. Plan a golden moment with someone now!

# Conquering Fear on the NYC Escalators

*I* have a fear of escalators. Well, I said it. I seriously have had this crazy fear of riding on those awkwardly moving stairs for quite some time. Now, if the escalator is in between tight spaces, I would go up merely holding my breath with very little fear. However, if there is complete open space, no way. There is nothing rational about this thought process, just an odd fear that I have allowed to consume my subconscious mind. And another thing, if the escalator is really tall, nope, I wouldn't do it.

One time at the mall with my son Ryan, he went down the escalator at a store, and I chickened out at the last minute and ran to find an elevator. It took me forever. This was really becoming an annoying fear for people who were running errands with me. It's even embarrassing to admit this goofy hang-up, but I do have a punch line at the end of the chapter, so stay with me now. Don't skip ahead to the end! Resist!

My chance to work on this fear showed up straight in my face while on a trip to New York City with Maggie and her best friend, my second daughter, Ally. We were thrilled to stay with my brother-in-law and his family in New Jersey. I cherish time with family and learned from Tammy to seize the moment and travel, visit friends and family, and dare to venture out. I will miss the trips she and I can no longer have together, but I am grateful for all of them that are stored in my heart. Thanks, sis, because I am inspired by you to do so much more of that now.

The girls and I sure embraced our time in the Big Apple. Our daily routine consisted of a daily 1 1/2 mile walk to the transit station and then a short ride on their rapid railway system, known as the PATH. Trekking from Jersey City to Manhattan, we walked an estimated 25 plus miles in four days and checked off many of our favorites on the long to-do list.

We saw two Broadway shows, *Finding Neverland* and *Fiddler on the Roof*, which my brother-in-law was acting in. We went ice skating at Rockefeller Center, a dream for a competitive skater (Maggie, not me) and a life-long lover of skating (this one is me - I actually loved skating and the Olympics so much as a kid that I begged to have the Dorothy Hamill hairstyle, popularly known as the "Wedge" cut) .

Gliding along on the famous New York City ice rink was pretty amazing. I grew up skating with my sisters on a pond and lake at our childhood homes. Dad was the best to clear all the snow off the ice, check its thickness, and put up lights for us to drift into the night on the smooth, clear sheet of glass.

The crazy and hilarious stories of our New York trip even made their way into a skit Maggie and Ally performed at a youth fine arts competition. Guess who was laughing the whole time? Me! I'm pretty sure they lost points because I was so loud; I was out of control.

My heart and face always light up when talking about that trip. One favorite memory was holding umbrellas in the rain at the NBC Today Show listening to Coldplay LIVE. I never knew about this band until hearing a CD in Tammy's car while my sister Tracey and I were driving in it on a trip. We popped in a CD and the song "Viva la Vida" came on. "Live the Life" perfectly describe our sister.

My NYC buddies and I took in all the sights and sounds (shops stayed open until 2am!!), eating at the best diners, and making new friends. In a big city like Manhattan, could you imagine running into the same group of people three times?! That happened to us. We met a nice group of friends while at Hillsong Church NYC, and ran into them two more times at the Today Show and by the Statue of Liberty. We even took a picture and exchanged numbers; we gained new friends from somewhere in the big state of Texas.

Let's finish the "fear" story, because you are probably on the edge of your seat by now. At every subway station and in every store, there were tons of escalators. At the Nike store, Forever 21 store, GAP store, subways, everywhere. There were 4-6 levels of escalators in some of those places. I needed to be sure to stay with the girls, and trying to find elevators each time was not in our very tight time schedule.

Throughout my adult years, I have faced some extremely fearful times and learned that facing the fear is really the best way to overcome. I once read a book titled, *Feel the Fear and Do It Anyway*, by Susan Jeffers. She says, "If something is troubling you, simply start from where you are and take the action necessary to change it. ...And you know that you don't like the fact that the lack of trust in yourself is stopping you from getting what you want out of life. Knowing this creates a very clear, even laser-like, focus on what needs to be changed."

Change. Overcome. Fight. Focus. Defeat the fear. Feel powerful hope and strength when you begin to resist the urge to stay below your potential. That was my mindset on the NYC trip. When we were on a big escalator, I held Maggie's hand and said a little prayer. Yep, I used to hold her tiny hand, and now she was holding mine. Again, I know this sounds silly and quite ridiculous; most fears are completely irrational. But, they are real and consume our thoughts and emotions. The escalator fear wasn't one of those lifetime fears by any means; it had been a recent oddity.

My tactics worked to overcome that crazy fear. Repeatedly going on those moving stairs (up and down, up and down) REALLY helped me to get used to them. I even started to like it and have fun!

That thrill of doing something I once dreaded became a game to me, and I wanted to win. I don't like losing board games ever. I like winning games, even if I must cheat now and then. Confession alert: I did cheat a lot in the game Sorry with my sisters when we were younger. I promise I do not cheat in games anymore, unless somebody is disrupting the game and creating chaos. Then, I can't apologize for what I will do to win the game.

Today, there may be an escalator here or there which may cause a little anxiety to quiver in me, but I know beyond a doubt that I can do it after so many successful times in NYC! Disclaimer: Though I did go on a ton (a ton!) of escalators on our trip, I will admit that often I took the stairs going up, and NOT because of a fear, but purely for exercise. Plus, I really liked beating the girls to the top every time!

Just as when we work muscles, there is pain. However, the growth of that muscle in the strengthening process becomes the prized treasure, leading to a fit and healthy body. The prize to overcoming a fear is the victory in itself. When we feel free and no longer a captive to fears and worries, the feelings of peace and confidence radiate throughout us. We cannot accomplish that without some discomfort and pain, just like the worked-out muscles.

Nobody wants to experience pain or discomfort, but I think there is no better feeling than to come out of that that time with new perspective and boldness. Overcoming fears makes room to reclaim that joyful hope. There is no easy, microwave oven fix with fears. Nobody will send you a golden ticket to immediately wipe out a fear of any kind. You'll likely have to face it and work through it. I think a great strategy is to grab a buddy and start going on those escalators, up and down, up and down.

\* \* \*

### Hope Follows fear

\* \* \*

*"For God has not given us a spirit of fear, but of power and of love and of a sound mind."*
  *2 Timothy 1:7*

**Big Idea** - Write down one fear you want to overcome; ask someone to help you face it with courage.

# A Distracted Mouse

*S*itting at my backyard patio table, ready to type, I heard
a variety of birds calling for one another, the breeze
dancing with the leaves on the trees, my wind chimes,
and a car alarm. Yep, it was so peaceful, and then a loud,
annoying alarm on someone's car blasted into my much needed
quiet time. Now, I don't mind the local car wash sounds and the
airplanes above, because I am used to those, but the long-lasting
car alarm?!

Maybe you can relate. After making the effort and time to
prepare for a restful moment, the phone rings or the doorbell
demands attention. There is a leak in the irrigation in the yard
spouting up five feet high. What is that weird sound coming
from the pool? The children are getting tired, hungry, and
restless. The dog just had an accident on the rug. The list of
interruptions appears mountainous compared to a little fifteen
minute break.

This reminds me of another time I was craving some relaxation. I was headed to a Yoga class at a nearby church; upon

arriving, I found out that I mixed up the class times. No class at that time. I was so disappointed! I wanted to just lay there and stretch to the beautiful music. So, you know what I did!? I grabbed my mat with all the determination within me and headed to a grassy park with shady trees. Ahhhhh, I found my spot. I spread out the exercise mat and had my own little relaxation and stretching class. Suddenly, I heard the sounds of men and lawn mowers! You guessed it; the landscapers arrived at my stretching class! And I wasn't even a trained instructor. I laughed hysterically and ran away as quickly as possible so they wouldn't spot me.

Immediately, I called Tammy, because you have to share those crazy moments with someone who has them, too. We laughed at the comical events of my morning. Kurt's sister, Karen, taught him when he was younger that if you can't laugh at yourself, you leave the job to everyone else. I love that! We often share that quote with our children; because when they have an "oops" embarrassing moment, sometimes it helps to take it with a grain of salt and chuckle.

After I got rid of the lawn mower distraction and made a dash to my car, I started thinking more about distractions. They happen whether we find them or they find us. I am very much like the mouse in the children's book *If You Give a Mouse a Cookie*, where the boy's pet mouse is hugely distracted. The mouse wanted a cookie and glass of milk, but he spent an entire day completely off task. In his defense, he did trim his hair, clean house, draw, nap, and more.

My typical day of distraction looks a little different from the mouse. I see a window that needs to be cleaned and get the glass cleaner; I put shoes away and reorganize the entire shoe area; I realize I hadn't swept the tile floor recently in the laundry room and end up sweeping the whole house; I fold laundry and find myself rearranging a sock drawer.

Imagine how I prepare for some relaxation time. It is more like a major event, and I wonder if you have the same challenge. Preparing for my relaxation time takes about 30-45 minutes. I gather some items (book, journal, pen and highlighter, beverage, and snack), put on comfy clothes, and tend to the dogs' needs; then, I finally sit down. Now, those things actually take about 5-10 minutes, but it is the DISTRACTIONS I listed above that derail my agenda.

I am improving with the distraction issue, but I can't deny how crazy and fun it is all at the same time. Many things get done, and I am forced to relax out of pure exhaustion. It does drive my family a little nuts watching me. I learned from my Lifestyle Coach for Moms, Holly Rigsby of *Everyday Joi Community*, to make a schedule and put my day into blocks. Prepare the next day's to-do list the night before. This is working wonders for me!

In order for us to have valuable and healthy relaxation time, why not schedule it into our week. In addition, claim some random, spur-of-the-moment relaxation time here and there. Whatever relaxation looks like to you, don't underestimate the power of its benefits.

*Northshore University HealthSystem* wrote an article about the techniques and benefits of relaxation.[2] "We're getting serious about stress relief. When people talk about relaxation, it often seems like something that we aren't always able to fit into our busy schedules. In reality, relaxation can be one of the healthiest things to incorporate into your everyday life. Daily stress can take a toll on both physical and mental health. Studies show that various forms of relaxation can help reduce many chronic health concerns as well as restore energy and encourage a more positive sense of self." The article listed popular relaxation techniques such as deep breathing, meditation, Yoga, muscle relaxation, and visualization.

Dr. Mina Lee Ryu, MD, FACP, *Internist in Internal Medicine at NorthShore*, listed some of the many benefits to weaving some relaxation into our days:

- Decreased heart rate and respiration rate
- Lowered blood pressure and increased blood flow
- Decrease in anxiety, depression and insomnia
- Relaxed muscles
- Reduced pain (long-term illnesses, chronic conditions)
- A boost in energy and better sleep patterns
- A sense of calmness and confidence
- Improved coping abilities

One benefit I personally find with relaxation time is that my "nice and happy" meter goes way up. Without a doubt, I am a happier and nicer person when I have had some "me" time to relax. I am better equipped with a calm disposition to take on the many hats I wear as wife, mother, teacher, writer, sister, daughter, friend, and more. I bet you feel the same.

I recently found a new way to get 100% relaxation time: dental work! The day of writing this chapter I didn't have to worry about distractions. You see, half of my face was numb. I knew for sure that I could gather my items (and avoid running around the house doing other things), because I needed to lay low and not chew on my numb cheek and tongue.

Thanks, amazing dentist, for the excellent work done on my

teeth and advising me to relax the rest of the day. I much prefer a massage or eyebrow wax for a bit of "forced" relaxation time, but if going to the dentist was what it took at that time in my life, then let it be. As I wrote away, feet propped up on the couch, I sure dreamed about when I would be able to eat food without a numb mouth: cookies and milk, of course!

\* \* \*

### *Hope Follows distractions and stressful moments*

\* \* \*

*"Be still, and know that I am God; I will be exalted among the nations, I will be exalted in the earth." Psalm 46:10*

**Big Idea** - Resist the urge to do several tasks at the same time. Focus on one. Then, go grab some cookies and relax!

# Living My Childhood Dream

T he list is made for mom and kids to venture out on the big shopping trip for school supplies and new school clothes. After three trips to five stores, someone forgot to toss into the cart a pencil pouch and lined note cards. One more trip, and who cares if they cost more at the local drug store; convenience and store hours are all that matter at this point. Can you relate? As a child or as a parent, I am sure this may jog the old memory bank. I loved the "Back to School" shopping season as a child; as a parent, I got to relive those days.

I used to take all my children at one time to get their supplies, which took a couple of hours. Then, there were years I tried something new and took them one at a time for some quality shopping time. One year, back to school shopping was different for our family.

After 22 years of being a stay at home mom of our four children, I took the plunge into FULL TIME teaching!! Technically, my position is .75 full time, but who counts the endless hours of work in a TEACHER'S life? Back to school shopping included my own teacher shopping list that year, and I couldn't have been more excited.

First, I need to tell you about my early childhood dream to be a teacher. You could always find me helping out a teacher or the librarian when I was in elementary school. I even loved playing school when I was younger like many girls. After my friends and I came home from "real school", I made several copies of some made up homework assignment using carbon copy paper (before printers were an at-home every day appliance). I set up the papers, supplies, and the huge chalkboard my dad bought me. I was ready to teach! It didn't matter that I was in 4th grade; I knew I was more than qualified to expand my friends' knowledge as their "after school teacher"! Okay, so that lasted about a half hour, and then they would beg to go outside to play. So, I gave in to their wild antics of being a kid after school and joyfully followed them outside to explore and play. Thanks to all my childhood friends who played school with me!

At the time of writing this chapter, Ryan and Jack were in college as a freshman and senior, respectively. Evan and Maggie were in high school as a freshman and senior, respectively. And no I did not accidentally repeat myself with the grade levels; those are actual facts. That whole school year was a ball of fun. However, as we edged towards springtime, I was knee deep with planning two graduations and preparing for Jack and Alexandra's wedding. Can someone make me a t-shirt to showcase that I survived that exciting, hectic, memorable, and costly milestone?

Before the school year with my two freshmen and two seniors approached, I started evaluating my life in the work place and how that would look. What could I do? What do I want to be when I grow up? Recalling how teaching was on my life "dream" list as a child, I ventured into the application and interview path. I had a blast! Applying to three different schools, and several interviews later, God put me in the best spot. My title: Elementary Communications Teacher for grades one through six. The best part about the job was the location. Sure, it was a mile from my house, but it was the school that Maggie and Evan attended. At least one of the three of us was super stoked!

I continue to find great satisfaction teaching a variety of creative and practical lessons on listening, speaking, and other important skills. I see 140 students every day and 470 students over each quarter. Here's the punch line: after working as a substitute teacher for nine years, I said if I ever taught full time it would be high school grades. I was passionate about pouring into the lives of teenagers and had a natural connection from my days working in Youth Ministry.

High school was not God's plan for my life, and now I cannot imagine teaching any other age group. I love my job beyond my wildest job dreams. I love my students and watching them grow more confident in how they communicate and share. Be careful what you say you won't ever do, because it may just be the thing God is preparing for you. I think God enjoys putting us into places that are way out of our comfort zones to watch us grow and change into better people.

Moving into new careers and callings, there is a period of transition and adjustment as you probably know. DID I EVER HAVE TO ADJUST!!! My free-spirited days included hiking, cleaning the house, running errands, sitting by the pool with a book, journaling, shopping, enjoying lunch with friends, and attending Bible studies. The shift to working early every day was exhausting like all working parents know. I learned to balance my long "to do" list, quality family time, and "me" time, but it was a new skill that did not come easy to me and had a huge learning curve.

On the other hand, I have learned so much and have grown as a person in my new career. Achieving and maintaining some form of balance came down learning acceptance and contentment. Here are four GIGANTIC lessons I learned going back to work full time at age 48, after a long sabbatical at home with children:

- Dust will always be there. (*I just don't stress about the mess anymore.*)
- Knowing the true meaning of "good enough". (*Enough said!!*)
- Utilize and appreciate your support crew. (*at home and on the job*)
- Be intentional. (*Focus on finding and seizing the meaningful moments.*)

The year 2020 brought on some overwhelming and unprecedented changes for our world. The pandemic Covid-19 stay-at-home orders created a need for remote learning in our schools. Every day, I saw my students on a Zoom video call, and I couldn't stop telling them how great of a job they were doing. I told these little heroes how proud I was of them and how they were rockin' that unique form of education big time! They missed their friends and teachers. Technology wasn't always smooth, which was an understatement. Parents, students, and teachers were frustrated beyond imaginable. It was just plain hard.

The students of that era, younger to older, will be a couple of very resilient generations in those unusual times. Be sure to compliment and affirm students you know and see. They need us to be their biggest cheerleaders.

Go ahead and take some time to dust off your childhood dream list. Sit and think on that for a bit. Jot down some ideas on paper or type it into the "notes" app on your phone (as my tech-savvy kids do). My hope is for you to pursue some wild and crazy childhood dream! I know being a teacher isn't really considered a crazy or wild career, at least most of the time it isn't, but I am being stretched and growing by leaps and bounds. I wouldn't trade it for anything!

\* \* \*

### Hope Follows lost dreams

\* \* \*

*"Delight yourself in the Lord and He will give you the desires of your heart." Psalm 37:4*

**Big Idea** - What childhood dream could you possibly dust off and pursue? Go make that list and show it to someone.

# Finding Gratitude on the Uphill

*L*iving in Arizona, we have some great universities for my children to choose for their post high school aspirations. I totally would have supported them going to college in Chicago or Indiana, a fine opportunity for me to visit family and friends and see the Cubs play baseball. I'm not really sure why they didn't want to look into out of state college options. Maybe they just wanted to stay close to home, near their siblings. Likely, they also wanted to save money and couldn't bear the thought of not having Mom nearby to drop off homemade cookies and to clean up their bathroom. Truthfully, I'm pretty happy that three of my kiddos chose to stay in Arizona, and one more will most likely follow suit.

Traveling away from home for extended visits wasn't something my children did, either, besides week-long mission trips. They stayed busy as teenagers in the summers with friends, their youth group and part-time jobs. But, one summer, Ryan had an incredible opportunity as an intern at a Christian youth camp in Prescott, which is about two hours north of Phoenix.

He is my independent child, who was the only one of my four babies to arrive ON their due dates and to completely open his eyes when he was placed into my arms after birth. He blinked and stared right into my eyes. OH, my heart melted. Those deep blue eyes and light hair, with such a calm and laid back spirit. Ryan is our phlegmatic, go-with-the-flow, middle-born son.

I know Ryan learned some amazing life skills that summer, and we were super proud of his adventurous and servant spirit. I did my best to support and encourage Ryan in that opportunity, but I had no idea three weeks could feel like three months! Maybe you have had someone move away from you for a short time, a sibling or child, and can relate. It's hard to be away from people you love and live with.

Because of Ryan's independence and complete focus, he will dedicate his whole self to a project, and that camp was no different. I hardly heard from Ryan, and that brought on some tears and learning moments for myself. Ugh, why does the light have to shine on our imperfections in those times!

- Julie's lesson #1: I had to learn a lot of patience and know that Ryan loves us regardless of the number of times he called home. There was no correlation. Okay, I got that. But to accept it, that was harder than ever. All four of my kiddos are different, but most of them do keep in touch with me when they are away. Well, I found myself crying several times, missing Ryan intensely, and wondering about his love and care for his family. God really let me know how foolish that was of me. I was stuck in my selfish thoughts, not opening up to all the thankfulness of Ryan's leadership experience.

- Julie's lesson #2: As God typically does, He shows me something I need to hear at just the right moment. I was reading a Bible devotion about *declaring our gratitude more than declaring our complaints*. Wow, that was me for sure. I had complained constantly about Ryan not calling or communicating with his family during those three weeks. You could say I was a little overly occupied with not hearing from Ryan. That is a huge weakness of mine, overthinking things. What a waste of time and totally not what God wanted me to be doing.

I decided to give God's idea a try: **give thanks**. I thanked God for this opportunity for Ryan, for the leaders who selected him, for the Pastors speaking at each camp, for the worship experiences and new friendships. I grew thankful for Ryan's hard work and dedication. As you can guess, my heart couldn't contain hopeless and negative emotions with sweet and gracious ones. One emotion side would prevail. I was elated to see how GRATITUDE could really change our hearts and minds.

During Ryan's internship, we drove up for a quick visit with him. What a blessing to see my boy and give him a big hug. I couldn't ask for anything more. While on our day trip, Kurt, Evan, Maggie and I had a great time exploring on our mountain bikes and delighting in some refreshing ice cream on that hot 95 degree day (*115 in Phoenix, so we were glad to be up north!*). It also happened to be the first time my children tried candy cigarettes. Dad couldn't help himself, reliving *his* childhood!

The mountain bike ride, however, pushed Maggie and me quite a bit. The trail Kurt picked was beautiful but extremely uphilly. Yep, uphilly, is my new word. It means "*uphill terrain that can be hard and exhausting when climbed on a bike"*. Maggie and I are not riders like the guys, but we took on the challenge in that blistering heat. We rode and stopped for breaks, repeatedly. But, when we finally got to a point at the top of the mountain, and ready to finish the trail, there was the most spectacular view.

Our eyes stared at the golden nugget: an open field with mountains and boulders beyond. It was as if we had to ride all that way just for this view, which is actually what happened. I had to admit that Kurt did take us on a cool trail, despite the difficulty. Besides the beautiful vistas, the best part of the actual trail was the DOWNHILL ride. *"Ahhhhhhhhh, this is wonderfulllllllllll,"* Maggie and I screamed with glee. I think she and I sang all the way back, which was much better than all the complaining happening on the uphilly parts.

How many times in life is something so hard for us to overcome; then, afterwards, we look back in surprise at the accomplishment and growth? The list of hard moments in our lives is endless: starting a new job; moving to a new town; starting college; working through a poor health diagnosis; dealing with a torn relationship, sending off a child to college; running a marathon; grieving loss; and birthing children, and the list goes on. Just when it seems so hard and you can't go anymore, that is when we can make a switch from hopelessness and exhaustion to gratitude and hope.

My friend, Sonia keeps a daily record of things she is thankful for and has inspired me to do the same. I have a small book I use to write down *three thankfuls* (a word I use to describe a list of thanks) each day. I do this every morning, and I don't write, "I am thankful for…" I simply write down the thankfuls. They can be small, big, profound or trite.

Some of my daily thankfuls are quite simple (no laughing, please!): post-it notes, purple pens, and highlighters. Another morning of thankfuls included my dogs, exercise ball, and yoga mat. Then, there are the deeper thankfuls: a fresh new year, new intentions, and new goals; Evan being a great friend and hard worker; Ryan taking good care of his rental home; Maggie growing in her confidence; and Jack and Alex's anniversary. Did you see that was four instead of three thankfuls? Sometimes, you'll find you have so much gratitude that you can't stop at three!

I even incorporated the *three thankfuls* into my 5th and 6th grade class. Each Wednesday for their Warm Up work, they write down their *three thankfuls*. Sometimes, we go beyond writing them; we share them with the class.

Try it out for yourself. I dare you to put on the hat of intentional daily gratitude. You will be a changed person in your heart and mind. Bonus: your positive outlook and disposition will become contagious to those around you. That's pretty nice for something that's free.

\*\*\*

### Hope Follows a discontent, complaining spirit

\*\*\*

*"Be cheerful no matter what; pray all the time; thank God no matter what happens*
   *1 Thessalonians 5:18*

**Big Idea** - Start a daily list of THREE THANKFULS! It's FREE!

# Beyond Your Comfort Zone

❧⊰❧

*D*o you ever feel so stretched and stressed out that you think your body is going to snap? I picture Elastigirl from *The Incredibles* Disney movie. After decades of being a momma at home full time, my new position as teacher did not start off all roses and butterflies. Standing in a classroom of students, I felt stretched beyond my usual routine of family management tasks. Weeks of planning, preparing, and organizing did not give me the full dose of confidence that I needed standing in front of 30 sets of curious eyes. (aka: my wonderful students)

Those first days and weeks were a ball of nerves. Thankfully, I persevered on, because I absolutely love my teaching job more than any other job I have ever had. I am grateful for my colleagues and friends at work; I love my school. What if I had decided to crawl back into my safe little shell like our desert tortoise, Amarri, and not push past the intense time in those early days of the new job? I would not know the rewarding life of a teacher; yes, rewarding, despite the challenges.

Fears and uncomfortable things in our lives come and go kind of like a swing moves back and forth. Do you notice that, too? Another time my fear muscle had some major work done was during the summer that Maggie embarked on a mission trip to Colombia with her youth group. What's the big deal about sending one child on a trip if the others have gone already?

Just as each child in a family looks different, there is no argument that their dispositions and struggles will differ, too. Maggie is very close to her family. As a baby, she was born two weeks early and quite needy. Truthfully, it was me, the momma, who became very needy with a 4 year old, 18 month old, and a sweet but high maintenance baby.

In the midst of growing up with three brothers, Maggie was total and 100% girl, playing with dolls, playing kitchen and restaurant, and starting up an at-home hair salon for the family; she was full of tons of "girly" energy. I loved it! Though Maggie was anything but quiet at home, she was more reserved and shy at school and other places. Living in a house with three adventurous and active brothers, it was hard at times to see our girl be on the more timid side when not at home.

Moving to a new school in 6th grade and making new friends was out of her comfort zone. Maggie was content with being at home with her family. As she got into middle school, she wanted to come home and be home schooled. We knew that would only cause her to withdraw more, and encouraged her to play volleyball and start a Bible group at school.

Leadership skills and new friendships began to develop at this point. Still, Maggie faced both typical and complex teen challenges along the way: friend issues, having worried and anxious thoughts, and insecurities. Many of my parenting years with my daughter focused on helping and equipping Maggie to deal with these challenges. Dr. James Dobson says it best about parenting with his insightful book, *Parenting Isn't for Cowards*.

What eventually drove Maggie to take first steps towards moving past her comfort zone was a vision she had at age 11. One day riding in the truck with Kurt, Maggie recalled listening to a touching song on the radio and having a vision or dream. It went like this: she was sitting in a circle with foster children and playing her guitar. The next part is profound. Maggie cried so hard at this vision. Her heart was touched like never before. We began to find ways to help her get involved with foster children in various programs.

Oh, the story doesn't end there. What a joy it was seeing Maggie fulfill a part of God's calling on her life. After Maggie saw her brothers travel on mission trips, it was her turn. She signed up with a close friend to go to Colombia and work with children and the community. As I looked into the trip, I saw the travel alerts and warnings for this particular country. In my moms' prayer group, I shared my concerns.

A friend said to me, "There are no travel warnings for God. If she is supposed to go, He will keep her in His hands." I loved that advice. I still was concerned for Maggie traveling so far and in an area of unrest, knowing the struggles she had dealt with emotionally. Would the stress cause her to panic? Maybe I should go along as a volunteer? Checking in with Maggie, she responded, "I'm good, Mom. I want to do this by myself." I nearly cried at hearing those words, at the confidence God was building up inside of her. And so began the "conquering of both our comfort zones."

Maggie went on the trip to have an once-in-a-lifetime opportunity helping in many community areas, and certainly with foster children. Maggie's vision and passion to help foster children were the fuel to help her stretch out of that comfort zone of staying close to home. I'm so glad she had that experience to minister, sing, and pray for the Colombian people. Unfortunately, the mission team faced some pretty heavy challenges. At one point, they were not allowed back to a place where they were staying due to an increase in street protests. Oh, did I get nervous.

I called upon my prayer partners and spent a night worshiping and praying for safety and provision for this ministry group. To add to the discomfort, Kurt was in Indonesia for two weeks. I felt alone and helpless. "Oh, God, please keep my girl and her team safe. Help them to continue ministering to your people there, despite the obstacles." It's a good thing God doesn't go on vacation from our prayer needs. God answered the abundance of prayers covering this team, and what an amazing trip it was.

Maggie shared her testimony of God's faithfulness and provision through our years of tragic losses. She shared this in a women's prison. This timid girl, turned into daring and confident, did something rare and selfless. She publicly professed the hope she found in the midst of our family's deep sorrowful loss, that God was her *waymaker*. My daughter stretched and grew, as did her Momma; maybe we can get matching Super Suits!

That trip increased Maggie's passion for God, prayer, people, and it allowed her the opportunity to form new friendships. Comfort zone – you sure had no hold on that girl! When I saw my baby girl walk down the airport terminal (*as I stood with a big welcome home sign, shaking and ready to attack her with big hugs*), I was taken back at how grown up she looked and acted. The calmness and confidence that only God could have instilled in her was beaming all over Maggie.

What amazing stories can God write on our lives when we get out of our comfort zones? Where can we go? Who can we reach out to? There is a saying Kurt and I learned in the years of building our Amway business. "Your greatest weaknesses will become your greatest strengths." I love Maggie's turnaround story. Her weakness of insecurities during the teen years radically transformed into a woman of great strength and leadership in helping children and the elderly.

At the writing of this book, Maggie is entering her senior year in college, majoring in Sociology with an Emphasis in Social Work and a minor in Counseling. I can't wait to see the route she takes with her experience and education. One thing is certain, it's a great thing she was stretched, because a whole lot of people will be helped by Maggie gaining new belief in herself. Let's not be afraid to stretch ourselves a little bit. Imagine the impact and influence you will have on others by simply not giving up. That is powerful!

\* \* \*

### *Hope Follows the uncomfortable*

\* \* \*

*"I have told you all this so that you will have peace of heart and mind. Here on earth you will have many trials and sorrows; but cheer up, for I have **overcome** the world." John 16:33*

**Big Idea** - Think of something that is out of your comfort zone. What tiny thing can you do to take a big step moving into a new direction?

# A Party in Your Mouth

What an ingenious idea to create a "National Day" Calendar. I sure wished I had created that fun calendar. Every day of the year there are thoughtful and fun reasons to celebrate. As I perused through the list of clever festivities, I decided that October 1st would be my favorite of 365 days: *National Home Made Cookies Day*! I love homemade chocolate chip cookies, fresh out of the oven. Have you ever taken a bite of some amazing food dish or bakery item, and it is like fireworks just went off in your mouth?! Seriously! Your whole mouth has this crazy feeling like it just experienced a shock wave, and you might even have a little saliva fall out? I call that a "party in your mouth" moment.

Think about the autumn months in October and November, specifically, with candy corn, caramel apples, pumpkin pie, warm turkey and gravy, and juicy cranberries, to name a few. I can't handle it anymore! I want a Starbucks Pumpkin Spice Latte now.

Perhaps you have also noticed the marketing of "pumpkin

flavoring" is absolutely abundant (and getting a little extreme). There are pumpkin Oreos, pumpkin Twinkies, pumpkin pancake batter, pumpkin lip balm, and even pumpkin toothpaste! I haven't tried the toothpaste, but I do love pumpkin pasta sauce. How extraordinary life is with the senses of sight, touch, smell, hear, taste. Not everyone has all their senses working 100%, but to have any working at some capacity can be a party. I love parties, and I totally believe even our senses deserve a party.

Because my vision is quite blurry without contact lenses or glasses, I believe my senses of smell and taste are more enhanced. Now, I don't have any proof on this, but I really believe it. I can smell things from far away, and I think my family considers me to be partly "super", as in Superman type qualities. My sense of taste is so strong, and when I eat something that has a lot of flavor, I feel the party going on right there inside my mouth.

With this keen sense of taste, I am often the guinea pig for taste testing leftover foods. My kids will ask, "Taste this, Mom, and tell me if it's ok." Sure, let me try the peculiar smelling food item. It's my pleasure as your mother. Maybe I should actually clean out the refrigerator more often and toss out expired foods. I am notorious for having unusual sightings in the refrigerator and am often asked to be the daring person who "tastes and tests" the freshness and flavor of the older food.

What areas of your life are more enhanced, due to another area being depleted or lacking? We are going a little deep here, but stay with me. When a tree branch is cut off, it will have a new area of growth. It will lack for a season, but then it flourishes. In our seasons of struggles and trials, do we grow stronger somewhere deep within only to be able to help someone facing that same challenge later?

Have you lost a pet? Then, do you share empathy with a friend or family member who loses one, too? Nobody can truly relate to specific struggles except someone who has walked in those same shoes. Kurt and I both had mothers who were widows and single mothers. We find ourselves being more sensitive to the needs of single mommas. Are those who once struggled financially more sensitive to those in need, because they remember the hardship and uncertainties? Are we more compassionate to a person who is homeless, because maybe we know someone close to us who has sadly been down that road? Does a bullied child tear at our heart strings, because we were once a victim of bullying?

Do we take time to sit and listen to a teenager who is struggling, because we, too, once were in that season of doubt and awkwardness, filled with confused emotions? Do we express love and encouragement to someone mourning the loss of their loved one? In my grief of losing my dad when I was 16, and then losing Tammy out of tragedy, I hold grief ever so close to me. It is one of those areas I have been through, and I long to reach out to others who are grieving. I will go into autopilot and send a note or card, share a prayer, or offer a hug. Everything within me wants them to know there is hope in the aftermath of their storm.

Think of areas in your life where you have experienced a personal struggle, and consider how you can turn it into a way to help others. Kurt, being an adopted child, has helped steer our family into places to help foster children. Having no family living near us in Arizona while being a young mom of four children gave me motivation to develop a variety of friendships to find encouragement and support. Now, as a veteran mom in my town, I'm ready with a list of referrals for anyone new to the Phoenix area. I suddenly put on the "Welcome Wagon" hat, offering suggestions for schools, doctors, and other professional services. I can't help it! I love meeting new people and helping them to get connected.

People all around us face challenges that quite presumably may cross our paths for a reason. We could be a tremendous breath of fresh air to them. Our words or actions can be a party to their senses, feeling our care and love. We have the privilege of sharing our unique experiences as encouragement to family, friends, co-workers, neighbors, and anyone we come into contact with.

Maybe it's fall for you right now or not, but pumpkin anything is perfectly legitimate any time of year. The last time I enjoyed something pumpkin-like was a delicious, unique pumpkin facial and hand treatment! Yes, I even smelled like a pumpkin, but if it made me look younger for a week; I'll take it 52 weeks a year! Allow those heightened senses to work for you in ministering and caring for people around you. There is someone just around the corner waiting for you, yes you, to be that inspiring hope to them.

\* \* \*

### Hope Follows personal struggles

\* \* \*

*"The Christian who is pure and without fault, from God the Father's point of view, is the one who takes care of orphans and widows, and who remains true to the Lord...." James 1:27*

95

**Big Idea** - Go ahead and eat something yummy, tasting the flavors one slow bite at a time.

# Carpe Omnia

As my children grew up and held part-time jobs along with keeping busy school and extracurricular schedules, we found it more challenging to get together on weekends for extended moments of family time. Aha! I had an idea, and Kurt bought into my sneaky and clever plan. On one Thanksgiving Eve, we departed the United States for a little four hour road trip to Puerto Penasco, Mexico (known as Rocky Point). Of course, when Kurt and I traveled there in the early 1990's, we set up camp on a deserted beach. Hotels were minimal with abandoned-looking homes as the only rental option. We opted for cheap, staying on the beach.

The children were not thrilled with going away from home for a big holiday. "Too bad," I declared, "Carpe Omnia!" which means *seize it all*. That is pretty much my life motto. I always had the knack for arranging successful, memorable trips, parties, and celebrations. I can't help it; I love to party! Living a "Carpe Omnia" lifestyle, I grew more intentional after the first years of losing Tammy. No border could keep me from seizing an opportunity to get away with my family.

Carpe Diem (*seize the day*) is commonly used to refer to golden moments. Nothing against that epic Latin phrase, but sometimes it stifles me. I know it doesn't sound fair to label that innocent phrase, but I want to seize more than just a day. It's the tiny moments at times I want to seize. It's the larger and grander causes and seasons of life I want to seize. Sometimes, I want to seize both at the same time. For those reasons, I can only live by this motto, "Carpe Omnia!" "Seize Everything!"

It seems to me that when we seize the tiny and larger moments in our days, our hearts will overflow with gratitude. I picture Carpe Omnia and gratitude wrapped together like a Reese's Peanut Butter Cup; you just can't have the chocolate without the peanut butter. Seriously! Can you even imagine biting into a cold, delicious Reese's, and as you take that mouthwatering bite, your teeth are in shock to find an empty center! NO Peanut Butter. I cannot even imagine it. Of course, if you are peanut intolerant like my son Jack, then this is not a good analogy for you. Maybe a York Patty is better. When we experience a "moment or more to seize", it automatically fills our hearts with immense gratitude.

On that particular Thanksgiving away from home, it all started when my dear, longtime friend Tonya told me of her family plans to Rocky Point and suggested we come along. I jumped on the bandwagon. She must be a committed friend to be my matron of honor and having worn that purple, satin bridesmaid dress I chose for my wedding in 1992. A trip to Mexico with no distractions at home? I wouldn't be cooking all day while everyone is watching the Macy's Thanksgiving Parade? We can play card games and just hang out at the beach? Um, yes, we will go! "Carpe Omnia!"

As I shared our NEW and never-before-done plans to "move" our Thanksgiving Day to Mexico, I got a lot of pushback from the four gems of mine. Thankfully, Kurt was excited to do something different and hang out with our friends for a few days. These happen to be our friends we would camp out on the beach with many years prior, so maybe he was thinking he would relive his young adult years.

Mostly, the complaints from my children were about not being at our own home and eating at our dining room table. How we could think of having Thanksgiving in a different country shocked them. Had their mother gone mad!? Of course, if I were to listen to my children's reservations and concerns each time I planned some new activity, then we would never leave our home to have amazing, enriching experiences. I mean how many times can a child say they rode in their family minivan on top of a huge tow truck bed, in 110 degree temps on the freeway? But, if we didn't have our summer beach trips to California, then our transmission would never have broken down in the middle of the desert one summer. I mean, come on, these are life experiences and memories you can't redo! (At least, I hope not with that one!)

And you can probably guess that the children had so much fun on our unique Thanksgiving trip. Maggie was baffled that I would take them out of town with no agenda. Because I always had plans, a schedule, and a to-do list of fun and educational activities for our trips, Maggie asked upon our arrival to the lovely beach house, "So, Mom what are the plans?" My reply, "There are no plans. No agendas or schedules. Do whatever YOU want!" Well, pretty much where we were staying, they had only two choices: hang out on the beach, or hang out on the patio at the beach. I loved it!! This lady really surprised her kiddos and husband with this kind of trip. It was probably one of our more relaxing and peaceful mini vacations ever taken as a family. We needed that time away as a family; if it takes going to Mexico to have quality family time, I'd do it again.

One of the more memorable parts of that trip was Evan discovering a new hobby and sport: fishing. Tonya's son, Lukman, took Evan under his wing to teach him how to fish. They went beyond fishing from the shore, but they went out on a paddle board and inflatable tube. At one point, I could see from a far distance Evan paddling the paddle board, which was actually tied to the tube, and pulling Lukman, who was fishing. I laughed with delight at the sighting of this wonderful young man Lukman, who is from Indonesia, making memories with my young son. It was an Obi-Wan Kenobi and Luke Skywalker moment of mentorship and friendship. As the tide revealed more beach, they walked way out into the deep blue and warm ocean waters of the Sea of Cortez. Whether on foot or on boat, they were out there fishing all day long for two days.

As I gazed past the shoreline into the wavy waters to see Evan on that paddle board, I couldn't help but think of the stories of Jesus fishing with the disciples. I marvel at how much Jesus taught them about *faith, perseverance,* and *teamwork.* There was the time when they caught so many fish that the boat was likely to tip over! That's a lot of fish! In my head I thought, "Fill up *my* boat, God, with blessings and treasures from you, special moments." Indeed, that trip filled up my boat of great memories, and some hilarious ones, too. Tonya and I played a prank on the kiddos, but we were caught. I want my boat *so* full of special experiences that it overflows.

Think about your past "Carpe Omnia" memories. Which ones stand out to you? Your boat of memories doesn't have to stay empty. I hope you go out and seize everything. Seize it all, as you make new memories and fill up your boat! Make it overflow! Carpe Omnia.

\* \* \*

### *Hope Follows change and new ideas*

\* \* \*

*"This is the day that the Lord has made; let us rejoice and be glad in it." Psalm 118:24*

**Big Idea** - Plan a fun activity that you haven't done in a long time!

# How is the Bread?

*I* loved shopping at the mall when I was younger. My favorite thing to do with my friends as a pre-teen was to be dropped off at the Southlake Mall to spend money on clothes and food. The warm pretzels were delicious and the steak fries at the New York Steak House were unforgettable. Of course, the best part of our mall adventures was the arcade. Centipede was my game of fame.

If you grew up in the 80's, then you know the iron-on t-shirt store. The walls were plastered with designs. You would buy the iron-on of your current obsession and the t-shirt. Then, you walked around the mall some more while you wait for your purchase to be ready for pick up; typically, the wait was one hour. Sometimes, we came back early just to watch the process of the huge, scorching hot iron press and to be sure they did the job to your liking. The 80's sure knew how to make clothing statements.

Once I was of legal working age, 16, I worked near that same mall at the movie theater. Apparently, I really liked the mall so much that my next two jobs after the theater were in the same area, a department store and a pizza restaurant. You could say the mall was a big part of my life.

As a young parent, I enjoyed taking my children to the malls to walk around and shop. In Arizona, I enjoyed the indoor and outdoor mall experiences. Oh, but the best part of our mall experiences were the summer movie events at Harkins Theater. I fondly remember those weekly movie trips, packing up my young children in the car with our snacks.

Then, one day, as if it were overnight, my relationship with shopping at the malls changed. I didn't get quality time with the mall for many years. When I shopped for myself, it was not at the mall. To be honest, I didn't shop much at all for me! Going out of my house back then was about walking the dog with children in strollers or on little scooters, going to a park or nearby splash pad, grocery store runs, appointments, school, and other easy activities. For many years, the restaurants we visited were those with little play areas, not the sit down with full service type. But, that was just fine with me. Just fine indeed.

When my children were older, I rekindled the old friendship with my long lost friend, the mall. It also helped having a teenage daughter who brought me back to the malls. I enjoyed a job at Gap for a couple of years and treasure the memories working there and helping customers. I started on Black Friday of 2015, running around greeting and helping customers. Literally, running around! I think it's pretty cool when you can return to a job that places you in your element, even after 30 years. I love working with people and serving them, and retail provided the perfect setting at that time in my life.

I didn't really know when I started at Gap that I was looking for a "gap" to fill in empty spaces in my life. After going through traumatic grief and finding new healing moments, it is natural to begin a search for something new to try. In that season, I found retail to be my "wheelhouse" where I thrived. It wasn't uncommon for customers to share about their personal struggles with me. One time, a kind and quite emotional woman shared about her daughter's family moving to Russia. When tears came, I didn't rush off. I found it such an honor to stay with my customer and encourage and offer hope and understanding. That was the most rewarding part of the job, the customer was number one. They didn't want us to worry about anything on the sales floor except helping and greeting the customer. Re-stocking could wait. It was all about the people.

I don't believe we are in our jobs to merely work, get paid, and deposit the check. I believe we are given the jobs as opportunities to serve others as Jesus did when he was here. I emphasize that even a smile and warm greeting can make someone's rotten day look brighter. As tradition would have it, three of my children would have jobs in the mall at a restaurant. Not only am I proud that they worked at age 16 and gained great life experiences, but they were hard workers who were friendly and genuine to their customers.

With my children being busier in their teen years, I found more alone time to run errands and enjoy stops at cafes and coffee shops. One time, I was enjoying some delightful food on a quaint patio of a fine foods grocery store. As I was typing away working on a blog post, I enjoyed some soup and bread. I love bread. Fresh, homemade white bread that is warm with butter melting on the top.

Confession time: I am a bread snob. There, I said it. I totally admit it! Now that I am all "grown" up and not raising little children, I do enjoy some good meals that I don't cook and have to clean up after. Choosing a place to eat other than Asian or Mexican food, I always ask, "But do they have good bread?" or "How is the bread?" While perusing a menu, I love to savor warm, scrumptious bread and butter. I have some favorite spots and would love any recommendations.

By far the best part of bread at restaurants is when the server brings the warm, delightful baked good to us without requesting it. This makes me think of the words hospitality, initiative, and presentation. I can't help but think of Jesus as a first class example for these actions.

He received and gave back *hospitality* by washing the disciples' feet and dining with friends. Jesus was the ultimate example of *initiative* to be out there in the world among hurting people to love them, heal them, and teach them. Regarding *presentation*, Jesus was all about **His** presentation. No frills about what he wore or the words he used. He just presented himself in a situation that called for attention. He was present. He was there to give, to serve, and to bring hope.

How can we be that way with our family who we live with? I find *hospitality* comes easy to me when having friends and family visit on vacation or hosting parties, Bible studies, and prayer gatherings. But, am I as hospitable to my own family this way in my daily actions and attitude? Do I set up the dinner table and prepare a meal with my best effort for my family, placing fresh baked cookies on a platter as I would when a guest comes to visit? Do I greet my family with the same enthusiasm as the times our relatives fly here for a vacation?

*Initiative* is my middle name. At our home, I am the lady to start all the cool projects. As a sanguine, I continue to work on follow up and clean up; they are not my strong point with my easily distracted ways. One of Kurt's biggest pet peeves about me remains to be my lack of effort with cleaning up my projects right away. Honestly, I get distracted and move on to something else on my to-do list. I'm not lazy or don't care about the cleanup part of a fun project; I really just forget. Isn't that convenient; besides, Kurt does a better job at clean up than me.

What about initiative with the relationships in my own home? Am I making time for my husband and children, or am I too busy with cleaning or my own to-do list? Why not drop the duster and sit and watch Evan play that video game? That would probably speak volumes to him on how I care about what he likes to do.

When *presenting* myself, am I ragged or rested as I tend to my mom and wife duties at home? Do I take care of my health inside and out? Or am I falling asleep while they need me to help with an assignment, because I was up late playing "Words with Friends" or browsing social media apps on my phone?

We all fall short of God's perfect glory as imperfect people. How marvelous to know we can change and tweak ourselves to fulfill the roles God has given to us. In the midst of changing times in our lives, let's add some salty and sweet bread for more flavor into our family. Showing hospitality, initiative, and presentation in our homes first is a great investment into our "home team", those we live with and do life with each day. They deserve our best.

* * *

### Hope Follows complacency and lack of effort

\* \* \*

*"Jesus said, 'Throw your net on the right side of the boat and you will find some.' When they did, they were unable to haul the net in because of the large number of fish." John 21:6*

**Big Idea** - Make time to sit and be present with your family. Play 2 roses and 1 thorn: share 2 good things about your day and 1 not so great. Oh, and have some warm bread.

# Chronicles at the Laundromat

*T*he setting for the writing of this chapter: a Laundromat. Our washing machine was broken. Pushing in the lever with my finger or a pencil to force the "water fill up"mode to engage during the wash AND rinse cycles was getting a little old. As I waited for days on a repairman, I took matters into my own hands as I tossed piles of dirty laundry into my car, heading for the Laundromat.

Because I would most likely be setting up camp in the Laundromat for several hours, I brought along my pal, the laptop, to do some typing on my blog. I arrived at "Coin Less Laundry" with a puzzled look. That name really confused me, but I guessed it meant I would just use a credit or debit card. "Coin-less" means no coins, right? Wrong; their system ran on dollar bills and tokens only. Good thing I was prepared with some money in my wallet and didn't have to pay the $5.00 ATM fee. ** *BIG TIP here*: take dollar bills to the Laundromat.

I must say, I was like a kid in a candy store. Trying to find machines close together and wheeling around the basket cart was more fun than I had all week! Seriously! I amused myself by talking to other customers and watching some dramatic moments of soap operas on the television. Taking in this new environment with a child-like attitude helped to replace any otherwise complaining tone of this inconvenience. During my waiting time, I began to blog. I wasn't making time at home to write, and this seemed to be a good opportunity to not get distracted with housecleaning.

It was a season of my second child, Ryan, graduating from high school. I started typing away and reflecting on Ryan's childhood throughout the teen years. The joys and the rough patches combined created a symphony of memories for me. The struggles, small or big, that we face in life make the victorious moments even sweeter. We had our fair share of struggles that seemed to vanish when we came face to face with the sweeter moments.

When my children are seniors in high school, like many families, I enjoy putting together a slideshow of pictures that tell that child's story. Moments of costumes made out of anything found in the house, the variety of hairstyles in the teen years, and drum sessions at youth events are just a few of the memories I wanted to highlight for Ryan's slideshow. As I perused through the endless piles of pictures, I intentionally chose those that best show Ryan's own personality. I look for those "last" moments.

His *last* first day of high school, his *last* day before final exams, his *last* swim meet, the *last* SAT test, and the *last* Homecoming and Prom dances to name a few. Then, there was the last FCA (Fellowship of Christian Athletes) meeting he shared with the middle school students who looked up to him as a mentor. Another touching moment was the last youth night as a senior where he and his drumsticks contributed to creating a worshipful environment.

OH, but this *last* I had no problem bidding farewell to: "Hey Ryan! It's the last Monday for your high school career! Get up! School starts in 30 minutes! Really, Ryan!? You only have 5 days left to try and get up early!" With angry, slanted eyebrows I lovingly shouted these worn out words from afar.

Ryan may be the younger brother to Jack and older brother to Maggie and Evan, but he is uniquely and wonderfully made to be "Mr. Ryan." And so the story of Mr. Ryan begins. We have experienced some moments I don't want to ever forget, like the time he stuck a pea up his nose. We had no choice but to hit the road to the nearest Urgent Care Center. As I panicked, imagining Ryan having this small green object taking residence in one nostril for the rest of his life or needing surgery, I could sense the doctor laughing inside as he attempted to calm me down. The solution: pinch other nostril and push a big breath into his mouth. It worked!! Out FLEW the pea to its freedom!

When unfortunate things would happen to Ryan as a small child, like a broken toy or not getting an extra cookie, he would make this droopy comment, "Poor Mr. Ryan." It was precious!! During the middle school years, Ryan became "In the Tunnel Ryan". As one of his brilliant teachers described to me, "Sometimes these young people are in a stage of being in the tunnel. They don't really see how their attitude is affecting those around them. They are uncomfortable and unsure. They need extra love and patience." Well, when Ryan was giving us a rough moment, we began to sing our "In the Tunnel" song to lighten things up. It was a convenient song to use for many years when any of the children were in a weird stage; simply insert other child's name.

Later, in Ryan's mid-teens, he became "California Ryan and 2.0 Ryan". These were moments in his life when he was making decisions to change some not so great attitudes, habits, and routines. Ryan's turning points are so Biblical; too, because Jesus teaches that we can begin *new* each day and remove our old selfish ways. I could share more about life with my middle son, the hard and the easy, the struggles, and the celebrations. One of the most meaningful moments with Ryan came when he apologized for his behavior towards me during his teen years.

Those were not easy years for me with Ryan. For him to come to that point as a young adult where he recognized his rebellious attitude and thanked me for not giving up on him, spoke volumes to what kind of man this Ryan was becoming. He didn't finish high school with the grades he could have, but he didn't roll over and quit on his future either. Ryan was committed to making college better than high school. After one year of working hard to complete an application process and maintain high grades, Ryan was accepted into the Marketing Program at Arizona State. Back when I was in college, you could declare any major with minimal qualifications, which was good; because, I am not sure I would have been accepted into the Accounting Program today!

Ryan is a stronger person because of his tenacity to finish strong and set himself on a different path for his future. How often do we face something so hard and just want to turn around and give up. During such a time in my life, I once read a book called, *How to Deal With Difficult People* by Gil Hasson. I needed insight and skills in how to work with some business and family relationships that were very strained. Sure, I could have just quit that business or stopped talking to those relatives, but thankfully, I had some great mentors in my life to push me out of the comfortable Lazy Boy chair and not give up.

Do you see what happened? I was twirling around with dirty laundry and rolling carts at the Laundromat making good use of my time, writing. Don't be afraid to be inconvenienced, because you never know what can come out of an opportunity to be present or start working on a project that has been waiting for you.

\* \* \*

### *Hope Follows inconveniences and hard moments*

\* \* \*

*"Let's hold firmly to the confession of our hope without wavering, for He who promised is faithful..." Hebrews 10:23*

**Big Idea** - Make a short list of the positives that have come out of a hard season.

# Hammocks and Trees

*A*re you ever jealous of kids? Maybe sometimes? I mean, can you admit that the aspects of playing and no responsibilities in the childhood universe are pretty great? Let's look at this concept of life as a kid vs. adult. I picture it like the *Batman vs. Superman* movie. Kids showcase their black masks and capes, while parents sport their hair with a sleek wave on the forehead and red capes.

*Kid responsibilities* - make bed, wash face and brush teeth, get dressed, go to school, play, do homework (reluctantly), play, chores (reluctantly), play, eat, sleep, repeat. Of course, as children age, they do take on more responsibilities like a job, doing their own laundry, and keeping up with social media every half hour. That can be some tough work

*Adult responsibilities* - make bed, wash face and brush teeth, get dressed, go to work to earn money, pay bills, maintain and repair as needed - home, cars, electronics/etc. Then, there are laundry and meal duties, financial plans and burdens, and family situations to resolve, to name a few. For those who carve out the time for recreation and hobbies, you feel as though you won the lottery to do something else besides the "daily grind" of our work and home tasks.

What a contrast in lifestyles between a child and an adult. I almost feel guilty with all the fun I had as a kid while my parents were working hard at their jobs and on our house. While kids and adults both enjoy entertainment and fun, only one group actually does it more than the other. What is holding us adults back?

When my son Jack returned home after his second year of college, he brought with him the coolest, comfy hammock. The kids tied it up between two palm trees by our pool and took turns in the ultimate relaxation nest. Evan used it the most and was often found lying in the hammock with a book or his phone. At times he would just sit or swing with the most relaxed look on his face. Okay, now I had to remember that he had no huge responsibilities as a 12 year old. Evan woke up on the weekends and headed to the hammock. Evan came home from school and headed to the hammock. After dinner, in the dark, anytime, Evan was in the hammock. Maybe Jack could have made some money by renting it out to Mr. E.

I have to be honest; my jealous feelings were beginning to rev up. I'm not talking just a little rev, but a huge rev. My FOMO (Fear of Missing Out) engine was at max load. From my kitchen window (which is where I was most of my days when the children were all home), I enjoyed looking into the backyard (thank you, Kurt, for keeping it up so nicely) and watching the kids play. I couldn't see the hammock too well as it was off to the side. BUT, I knew Evan was in there. I could sense it like I was related to Spiderman and had "Spidey senses".

One day, I was determined to have a turn in that lovely, relaxing hammock. I didn't like feeling left out. I found the hammock to be quite comfortable!!!! I had no idea it was that comfortable, because it looked like Evan was wrapped up in a banana and scrunched together, unable to move.

As I lay there, I closed my eyes for a bit. Then, I opened them up to see the beautiful and large palm tree holding the hammock. I have always been fascinated by trees, especially palm trees. Some are skinny and tall, thick and tall, and others are shorter. I am so amazed at how God created this beautiful and strong tree.

When the palm trees are trimmed and cut down, I can feel the thick and sturdy make-up of the tree as I pull the branches to the garbage bins. They are super heavy. This led me to further awe at those palm trees. How do all those branches stay "plugged" into that TALL tree? Add the 20-40 mph winds we can have in monsoon season, and those branches and trees dance like there is no tomorrow. Nevertheless, they remain unmoved by what was happening around them.

This made me think of how vital it is for each of us to have someone to "plug" into, maybe a whole "team" of people. For me, I can't and don't want to face worries, stresses, challenges, trials, and losses alone. To be part of something bigger than myself is my secret. First, I have the strong and loving God, Creator of Heaven and Earth. So many times I have prayed to him, wept at my Savior's feet, seeking wisdom, direction, and comfort; grace and mercy from my sinful self. He is truly my anchor.

My main crew next to God is my husband, children, extended

family, friends, counselor and pastors. As I look at that tree, I think, "I am *THAT* palm tree." Those amazing people in my life are the branches holding me up. Could the branches be part of the foundation and strength to that palm tree? Is that possible? It sounds really crazy, doesn't it? I don't know, but I do know that God gave me that glimpse of hope, whispering, "Julie, they have you; they are holding you up." Thank you to all who have encouraged me and loved on me during the first years after losing Tammy. It meant so much, and I only hope to give support and care back to you.

Absolutely, kids and adults both have a need for a variation of a support team, friends and family you can trust. You'll find so much value in having a set of your own branches to hold you upright when facing times that shake you. We need our tight gang to come along side us when we lack in faith, trust, and hope. Just as we need our support team, consider the people to whom you play an important "supporting role". Offering support and receiving it can be easily done on the phone or via a text or letter. We all need encouragement and support!!! Identify your branches!

\* \* \*

### Hope Follows F.O.M.O. (*Fear of Missing Out*)

\* \* \*

*"Therefore encourage one another and build each other up, just as in fact you are doing."*
  *1 Thessalonians 5:11*

**Big Idea** - Take some time to lay in a hammock or even in a chair with your feet propped up. Look up at some nearby trees, pondering all the wonderful people in your life.

# I Spy Some Pretty Cool Blessings

ne day when the honeymoon phase of marriage begins to look a little hazy, you come face to face with some pretty strong realities that you weren't aware of back when "I do" was surrounded by butterflies and bubbles. In my new blissful teaching career, my honeymoon phase was coming to a close pretty quick after I started.

I was reading through a book that caused unsettling doubts and emotions to rise up within every piece of my body. Was I doing the right thing by not being home full time anymore? Will my children be okay with me not being available to them every night if I am working on school work? Will they feel ignored and not connected to me? This was a new hemisphere for me.

The poignant section out of the book *A Woman After God's Own Heart* by Elizabeth George read, "Now, by faith, I stay at home more often than I might naturally choose, keeping my home, trusting God to bless my obedience. Oh, I'm not home all the time, but I am there much more than I was! And there are many blessings!"

Honestly, the "stay at home more often" part brought about a flood of memories and tears. This described my life back in 1995, when I was about to have my first child. I had left my career as an Accountant and enjoyed my new job as Youth Director. YES, I know what you are thinking. Those are two completely different fields! There is no explanation other than during college I wanted something challenging to study and loved numbers; later, I had discovered a passion for ministry with teenagers. Two different jobs that I equally enjoyed.

The year 1995 represented a 22 year calling for me as a stay at home mother (Family Manager, to be official). Kurt and I made this decision mutually for our family, and we knew full well that even with Kurt's work as an established Engineer that finances would be tight. I had always dreamed and hoped I would be able to stay home with our children and beyond grateful for this experience. Emotions of sadness, thankfulness, and joy filled my heart.

Memories flooded my mind of all the days at home with my children during the seasons of infancy and childhood, homeschooling, new school, Little League and ice skating seasons. The collection of moments running around in my brain were varied: the fun times, the hard times, the times I don't even want to talk about, and the times I couldn't be happier. All those memories came upon me like a wave on the North Shore of Oahu.

After my emotional breakdown, I gathered myself to shift my thinking. I decided to change the wording from the book: "By faith I now am *WORKING FULL TIME*, trusting God to bless my obedience. I am not at work all the time, but I am at work more than I am home, now. And there are many blessings to name!"

Besides the blessing of doing what I love to do, TEACH, I absolutely treasure these children and watching them learn, grow, and develop new skills. How can your heart not melt when you walk through the school halls and see them moving their tiny index finger up and down like a puppet to wave hello? The cutest time ever was when one little boy kept looking forward, walking in line, but had his little hand held out far to the side "waving" that one finger at me like he was a secret spy.

Another blessing I discovered early on was my family's support. They pitched in to be more of a full on Olympic TEAM. There is no way I could have made the transition to a full time career without them. Thank you to Maggie for the cute notes you left on my desk at work when you snuck in during your Elementary TA duties and coming to visit my classrooms. The kids loved seeing you! Thank you to Kurt for doing more dishes than ever and the surprise visits with Pumpkin Spiced Lattes (DECAF) from Starbucks. Thank you to Evan for putting stickers and stamps on hundreds of worksheets for my students. Thank you to Ryan and Jack for being proud of this momma and pushing me to not quit during week one when I was lying face down on the front room floor, overwhelmed, sobbing, and ready to quit.

The silver lining blessing that I didn't anticipate was my new friends. In the first year, I shared a small, unusually shaped office with Elementary Spanish and Art Teachers. We had more laughs than I knew what to do with! My favorite moment was when I told them of an awkward crosswalk situation I experienced. As a crosswalk guard, I was very happy to see the children and parents and grandparents. Even when it was 100 degrees out, I kept a positive attitude as I said, "Good Morning", with a sweaty smile. BUT, one time, I greeted a mom and her daughter with, "Good morning, Lazies." YES! I called them LAZIES, instead of LADIES! I felt horrified and couldn't even speak. (I did apologize to them later.)

My teacher friends laughed at me, and then my Spanish teacher friend told us of a hilarious comment she made to someone during her crosswalk duty. BUT, the story that had us practically on the floor was from my Art teacher friend. She shared about something so funny that happened at her wedding. Instead of thanking her guests for being at her special day, she congratulated them! I wonder how many people she wished congratulations to before her new husband told her what she was doing. Oh, we laughed hard. Laughter is good food for the soul.

Besides laughs, we supported and encouraged one another, sharing our joyous and tough life moments, too. You really can't hide much in a small area of three women. And could we ever party! Bringing treats to the office, coffee shop runs and outlet store shopping were routine for us. Now that I think of it, did I make any money that year? I continued to grow in the blessings of friendships at school and share a unique and special bond with my fellow teachers.

My hope is that you will see the season of life you are in and be thankful as you point out the blessings and positives. Go on a little "I Spy" hunt and start with naming three. Consider three things in your current career, vocation, or calling that has brought you joy, peace, happiness, and even hope. You could even write them down now with the current date.

This is a great remedy for when you are frustrated or discouraged. Just pull out that list and read it over and over. Feel free to add to your list now and then. I am pretty sure we aren't limited to a certain number of blessings and intangible gifts. I bet God has you where you are right now for a purpose and season. By identifying the good things of your work, you will begin seeing more positive aspects around you.

\* \* \*

### *Hope Follows frustration and discouragement*

\* \* \*

*"I have it all planned out—plans to take care of you, not abandon you, plans to give you the future you hope for." Jeremiah 29:11b*

**Big Idea** – Make a list of 3 really cool things about your job.

# Oh, Christmas Tree

*P*arks are great places to not only walk around, but to contemplate life. I have had some of the most exhilarating and eye-opening moments when by myself on a leisure walk. Not only is walking great for our bodies, but it can be considered healthy mental and emotional therapy either when alone or with others. We often have time to ponder, think, and reflect when taking a walk alone; while when we are with others, it is a time to fellowship and encourage one another.

Another one of my walks with my dog Ellie, I was walking along a park trail and found myself standing by the fence that blocks the interstate traffic. I watched the cars zooming by and stopped for a bit to watch. The noise factor wasn't as bad as the visual of the cars. There were hundreds driving by, all kinds of colors, models, sizes; it became overwhelming.

Let's just say, hypothetically, I was part of a test group to track and record cars. Whoever gets the most recorded in one hour wins the prize. Picture me, rather picture my head, quickly moving left to right, right to left, back and forth practically getting whiplash. First, I would need to see each car; then, write it down. Repeat that a zillion times.

As I was staring with wide open eyes thinking about all those cars, I soon became tuned out. All the visuals and sounds fell on me like when Charlie Brown has a rain cloud over his head and nobody else. Dare I say that I felt captivated, or maybe captured. I couldn't move.

That's when it happened. Suddenly, I got a whiff of the pleasant, evergreen scent. What in the world was this? The month was December, but it was such a strong smell like that of a Christmas tree farm. Where was that blissful aroma coming from? As I looked around with Ellie by my side, I turned and saw the answer to my question! It was a gigantic pile of Christmas trees that had been dropped off for the city recycling and mulching program. Ahhhhh, that smell, how I love it.

This experience came back to me as I was reflecting on the 2020 Pandemic of the Covid-19 Virus. During the many months of stay-at-home orders and remote learners and workers, cars weren't really on the road too often. If I were to go back to the park and take that imaginary tracking and recording test again, I would have a bigger list and much easier time. My head would not move so swiftly back and forth. No whiplash, for sure. I would even be able to write legibly as opposed to scribbling when writing furiously fast.

During the pandemic, most people saw a lot of change and faced experiences and hardships like nothing in their lives up to that point in time. We learned new terms and methods to stay safe and healthy. We searched everywhere for toilet paper. We learned patience and resilience in a massive way. We stood in long lines for more toilet paper. We coordinated face masks with our outfits.

Sadly, we saw record breaking job loss, financial hardship, and dreaded mandates not allowing us to visit our senior family members or those with medical conditions. Come to think of it, the entire experience completely rocked our world and took us out to sea navigating a storm in the dreary, dark night.

When I think about those cars on the freeway, I realize there are going to be cars out there every day. Some days there are more, and some days there are fewer. There will always be people driving somewhere. People will drive at night. People will drive in the daytime. It's just like the 2020 pandemic year. We will always face hard things in life as I have spoken of throughout this book. But, our focus and perspective are capable of shifting to shedding light on what is dark.

As I turned to see those Christmas trees in a pile because I smelled them, I had to turn away from the cars and look at the trees. I walked slowly up to them and felt so small next to the huge pile. But, that is how the 2020 year was for us. We felt so small in our world, helpless and unsure. We were reminded to shift our focus if we didn't want to drown in the negative.

I submit to you that your life isn't supposed to be a fast paced freeway driving you to madness. You're not meant to be consumed with reading every article or listening to every newscast detailing the problems with that pandemic or any other unknown you may face. No way, you guys. Your life is meant to be saturated with hope-filled experiences and moments.

When you are bombarded with the negative around you and feel yourself drifting away and zoning out, take a deep breath. Turn around and pivot to get a new perspective. Find something good and positive to dwell on. What if we all started to do this more often, building up our resilience? What if we think a little differently?

Every school year, I begin my 5th and 6th grade class with a "Best Year Ever" unit. Through various activities, we study and break down what it means to have your Best Year Ever. According to author and "Michigan Teacher of the Year" Bill Cecil, teaching students to give their best ATTENDANCE, ATTITUDE, and EFFORT prepares them for success inside and outside the classroom. The students receive a coin with the words inscribed on them as a visual reminder to have their "Best Year Ever". The goal is for them to keep it on their desks during class as a reminder of the success that awaits them. The tricky part, of course, is to not play around with it or drop it on the floor. You can probably imagine all the "ching, clank, clink" sounds I hear in a class time.

I am often heard saying to my wonderful students, "Now, remember to keep your coin in the corner of your desk. I don't want to hear them. It's all about having your Best Year Ever." The principles of "Best Year Ever" can apply to our lives at home, at work, and at school. But, please, keep your coin on your desk.

\* \* \*

### *Hope Follows the unknowns*

\* \* \*

*"Humble yourselves, therefore, under God's mighty hand, that He*

*may lift you up in due time. Cast all your anxiety on Him because He cares for you." 1 Peter 5:6-7*

**Big Idea** - Read about Bill Cecil's story on having your Best Year Ever and give it a try.

# Did I Get Everything Done?

❧

*E*very year on December 30th, I have said to myself, "Aw man! Oh no! I meant to do this or that. I wanted to go here or there. I hoped I would have done something more." This odd self-talk session initially began as a serious form of regret. Then, over the years, I continued it as sort of a joke. Allow me to explain.

Do you find yourself saying those familiar "REGRETS ONLY" phrases about the previous year with wide open eyes glaring at the next day, December 31st, the last day of the year? Do you find yourself thinking you have this list of things to complete before midnight? I'm pretty sure this started for me when we began building an Amway business. At the end of each month, we made the push to get over the next point bracket and earn a slightly higher monthly check.

To set the record straight, December closings are certainly not all gloom and doom. Kurt's birthday is on December 31, and that is the best part of the end of the year when we celebrate and honor the man who takes such good care of me and our family. His brother has always said, "Kurt, everyone in the world is celebrating you!" What a great brother you are Karl! I love seeing my husband hanging out with his siblings. They are such a fun crew I am grateful to call my family.

I have an annual joke around here that as the clock nears midnight on December 31. I shockingly and loudly proclaim, "Oh no, you guys, I forgot to do something before the end of the year!" Then, I calmly respond to myself, "Oh well, it's too late." with a happy and sarcastic kind of tone. Oh, you have to admit that you talk to yourself, too. I said earlier that I don't really argue with myself, but at times may have been heard scolding myself with a little pep talk. When you are older, who is going to do the pep talks for you? May as well just set yourself straight now and then.

As our family begins a new year and fills out our usual goal setting sheets, we begin with reflecting on the past year experiences, changes, and achievements. Then, we turn our eyes onto the new year. It is time for us to set new goals for these categories: Spiritual, Physical, Financial, Social, and Educational.

This year, I felt a different approach to a new year. Instead of feeling briefly glum or disappointed for what I didn't do, I took time to look at all I did do. How I changed. The new traditions. The new seasons in our family. The friends I visited. The distance family I spent time with. Just as a person who sets goals to run a marathon must train daily, both physically and mentally, we can train ourselves to have a "mind shift" from one year to the next.

Okay, people, it's time to hit the brain treadmill: train myself to look at the good. I did not watch all of the *Anne of Green Gables* series for the 5th time with Maggie, or the entire *Star*

*Wars* movie collection with my boys, but I can train myself to look at what I did do with my family. We swam, hiked, and biked. We played a lot with our new puppy. We watched other movies and played games. Maggie and I started a new TV series we absolutely enjoy called *This Is Us*. If you like this show, you have to see Jimmy Fallon's behind the scenes video on YouTube. It is hilarious! (It may be sad, too, because of the content.)

The more I contemplated the things I did, the more they just rolled out of my head. We went to Dutch Brothers for cold drinks when the new café opened near our home. I enjoyed shopping with Maggie and Ryan for back to school college necessities. We took a dog obedience class with our new puppy, Darla.

Since Evan was the only child at home after his siblings moved out, it was time to start new traditions instead of basking in our misery of loneliness. I knew it would be a hard time, especially for Evan, so we created two new traditions. First, we started Taco Tuesday nights, where we take turns choosing a restaurant each week to find a great taco deal. I even found a shirt at Old Navy for Evan that says Taco Tuesday! What are the odds of that!

Our other new tradition we declared was a Treat Thursday, where Evan and I take turns getting a treat after school. These range from nachos at the nearby Mexican restaurant to root beer floats and shakes. I'm not really sure how Evan feels about being home with just Mom and Dad, but I am thoroughly enjoying it.

Among our funny antics around the house with just the three of us was the time Kurt and I were talking about something at dinner, but Kurt forgot where he was going with that conversation. Evan responded, "You old people need to get your stuff together." Would you ever laugh if this was the first born or middle child? No way! But, somehow it's hilarious with the baby of the family and how it came out.

We don't have to search far to find some amazing experiences and accomplishments. Do the search for yourself, and see what you DID do and see. See what changes you DID experience for the better. By the way, be ready to be super proud of yourself, because when you begin the journey of reflecting on the positive, the new proclamation will be, "Whoa! Look what all I did!"

\* \* \*

### *Hope Follows self-defeating thoughts*

\* \* \*

*"Jesus looked at them and said, 'With man this is impossible, but not with God; all things are possible with God.'" Mark 10:27*

**Big Idea** - Why not make another list?! List the five top achievements or experiences from your year so far.

# Don't Take Your Eyes Off the Mountain

Keep your eye ON the mountain. Sometimes you need to tell that mountain it will NOT take you down or defeat you. Sitting on the lanai outside our lovely condo bedroom in Kaua'i, Hawaii one summer, I was captured in the moment of such an unforgettable view of majesty and beauty. The tall mountains were being visited by some passing rain clouds and the sun was brightening up the landscape. It was our first time visiting the Hawaiian Islands and all I could do was stare at the majestic views outside.

I was reading Acts 4 in the Bible and deep in the drama of Peter and John. They were put into prison for doing the work of Jesus and healing a 40 year old crippled man (he had been crippled from birth). My eyes looked up from the words I was reading to take in this dramatic, historic event and picture how the priests were so unsettled by the healing. Yet, all the people around were praising God for this miracle. I can picture the priests looking at each other with a look that whispers, "What do we do here, guys? Everyone loves this Jesus and his buddies; gotta admit, it is pretty cool what is happening."

While I am snickering at the picture of this ordeal, my eyes looked up from the pages of this account to see something I didn't know how to describe. There it was, I saw probably the most breathtaking and stunning sight I have ever seen in my first 50 years!!! Those tall mountains in front of me with giant palm trees and other gloriously green vegetation had the most picturesque visitor in their setting! There was a wide, colorful rainbow against the mountains, stretching from the palm trees up to the sky. This was no ordinary rainbow!!

I jumped up from my chair and stared, and then I ran around the condo calling for everyone to come see it, "Hey you guys! Come here right away! You have to see this! It's so beautiful! Hurry! This is the most beautiful thing you have ever seen!" I was literally shaking. My body was overwhelmed with the sight of a most breathtaking rainbow. When everyone arrived on the lanai to see the sight, it was nearly gone. Vanished, I tell you! I sank out of sadness that they missed the big moment with *Kaua'i Rainbow*, my new friend.

The rainbow is full of color and bends from one part of the earth to another, reaching out to us. It represents hope. I remember when my Dad died and how my Mom would see a rainbow as her hope of moving into a new season with God as her helper and guide. She even started a support group at our church for grieving children with "Rainbows for ALL Children." When she later became a Camp Nurse in the summers, her nickname was "Rainbows"! My children fondly call her "Grandma Rainbows"; she continues to see this beautiful artwork by God as the peace of knowing He is with her in all the hard times of life; what a gift to pass onto her grandchildren.

Do you see why I say, *"Don't take your eyes OFF of the mountain?"* Did you notice how I jumped from the "beautiful and once in a lifetime sight"? Sometimes, we need to keep our eyes ON our "mountain". Mountains can represent many things to people, some of which are the most complex and difficult obstacles. Even in the Bible, Jesus says "speak to the mountain."

All this mountain talk reminded me of a time I spent with a woman who mentored me spiritually in my prayer life, also named Julie. She taught me to boldly SPEAK words of affirmation and words from the Bible. I learned to speak TO my mountains, the problems, fears, and worries. Developing a heart and mind shift, I told those mountains what they could do and where they could go; I would no longer allow them to dictate my outlook and attitude.

Putting it into practice, I have a very personal story to share of how I once got over a gripping fear. This was such a paralyzing fear that I felt I was held in hostage. Early in our marriage, Kurt worked evening shifts as an engineer. I was home alone through the night and would check several times that the doors were locked. Oddly, it went beyond doors. I actually would look in closets and underneath beds to be sure all was safe. I had never experienced something so unusual before, and the fear kept growing. One night was so bad that I thought I heard something outside the bedroom window. And what did I do? I got into my car and drove away to call my husband from a payphone (no cell phones). Now, how was that a safe idea?! It wasn't even rational! If someone was outside of the house, they could have jumped into my car.

I hated how terrified I felt and the constant "checking" the house for safety. What was I expecting to find, anyway? IF there was a crazy guy in a closet, was I prepared to kick him and karate chop him on the head or in the gut? Somehow, I traced this unusual behavior to my days of watching horror films with Tammy. We searched the shelves at the video store for movies based on the length of the film: the longer the minutes, the better the movie! That was our own rule. We watched so many scary movies and loved it back then! However, I think many of those scenes came back to haunt me. I do not watch those anymore!

Through help and guidance from some wonderful spiritual mentors, I began to move that scary "mountain" out of my life. My friend, Gloria, suggested I read the book: *The Tongue, A Creative Force* by Charles Capps. In the back of the book are Bible verses to read out loud in times of need (financial, physical, emotional, etc.). I am warning you here; I began to take position and battle the fear that consumed me. Each night instead of checking things in closets or beds, I spoke faith-filled scripture verses **TO** the mountain. I spoke loudly and demanded that fear be removed from me. I would not be ruled by some invisible and irrational feeling any longer.

The conclusion of this story: GOD moved that mountain for me! I praise GOD for freeing me from that distressing time in my life. But, seriously, nothing happened until I began to FACE the mountain and take ACTION towards eliminating it.

What MOUNTAIN are you facing? Who cares if it didn't get resolved in 1962, 1975, 1988, 2000, 2019, or even in 2020. Don't put a date on it. Just take action DAILY towards facing it and conquering it. Gloria, who I mentioned earlier, faced mountains and has written a book about one of them: *Stuff Happens: HOPE Anyway.* I highly recommend her book. Go forth and conquer your mountains! You got this!!

\* \* \*

### *Hope Follows impossible mountains*

\* \* \*

*"Truly I tell you, if anyone says to this mountain, 'Be lifted up and thrown into the sea,' and does not doubt in his heart, but believes that what he says will happen, it will be done for him."*
   *Mark 11:23*

**Big Idea** - Take a hike or walk and discover the beauty surrounding you. Consider what mountains you are facing and speak words of belief. "I am more than a conqueror and will overcome!"

# I Tell You, You are Great

*et's* play a little game: "Two Truths and One Lie". As a one-way game, this may pose a bit of a challenge. I love games and am pretty competitive. I have only cheated in one game in my life: "Sorry". When I played with my sisters as a child, I moved my pawn closer to my safety zone and moved their pawns further from their safety zones. It was glorious!

Here we go ~
    Truth or Lie: I have beat Kurt in a jet ski race.
    Truth or Lie: I was a cheerleader in high school.
    Truth or Lie: I am related to Abraham Lincoln.

Which one did you pick as the "lie"? By the way, I am only okay telling a "lie", because it is a game. Generally, I don't lie. Okay, now it is time for revealing the answers. Drum roll, please. #1 is a truth: Kurt and I raced jet skis at Lake Powell, and I won. I learned my sense of power-motor adventures from my dad on our snowmobiles. #3 is a truth: yes, I am related to

President Lincoln through his wife, Mary Todd. #2 is the lie: I was not a cheerleader. I did actually try out for the Pom Pom team in 9th grade and did not make it. I was disappointed but enjoyed my high school years working fun part-time jobs, learning about journalism on the school newspaper staff and plenty of socializing.

I bet you thought #3 was the lie and #2 was truth. Many people think the cheerleader statement must be true, because I am quite the friendly extrovert who loves to plan and attend parties and big events! I can create a celebratory event in no time with lots of hands on deck. But, I just don't carry even the slightest thread of dancing skills.

Though I am related to Mary Todd Lincoln, and from what I read, we do not share the same passion to socialize and host. She was a woman who was quite contentious. To have more of an appreciation for the intense time Abraham Lincoln faced with our country, I want to share a little information with you. I have recently learned some facts that make the historically favored president, Abraham Lincoln, all the more admirable and respectable. Allow me to retell what I learned from author Gary Thomas in his book *Sacred Marriage*.

One of the attributes Abraham Lincoln found attractive in Mary Todd was her aggressive and brilliant personality. The truth of the matter was she had an irrational and impulsive temper. Lincoln paid his hired help extra money just to keep them from quitting! One time, a salesman visited the White House and was greeted with Mary offering quite an unfriendly welcome. The man went straight to the Oval Office to complain to the president. Lincoln gently said, "You can endure fifteen minutes what I have endured for fifteen years."

As if a difficult marriage wasn't struggle enough, the Lincolns sadly lost their son Willie, which caused more intense turmoil and anguish for Mary. Here is a president dealing with his own personal trials, doing what he can to keep his marriage together, and still giving it all he has to keep a crumbling nation from falling apart.

The days before Lincoln delivered his ever famous speech in Gettysburg, another son had become very ill. Picture the fog Lincoln may have been in with all that was on his mind. From what I read, it sounded like he quickly jotted down some notes and rode on to Gettysburg. Later, he reflected on his speech, "It is a flat failure, and the people are disappointed." He couldn't stand his speech! This shocked me! He thought he failed miserably!

What a story to see the outcome of that speech, one of the most famous in history. The words he spoke were true and genuine, moving and powerful, despite *how he felt* he delivered his speech. What kind of person can endure all that hardship and go on to become one of the greatest presidents in our country's history?

Author Gary Thomas said, "Not only did Lincoln's difficult marriage not deter him from achieving greatness; one might argue that it actually helped prepare him for greatness. Lincoln's character was tested and refined on a daily basis so that when the true test came, he was able to stand strong. His spiritual muscles were strengthened to the point that he didn't falter just when he needed them the most."

To close out this book, I invite you to come along the journey of being an overcomer and a hope finder. Allow Abraham Lincoln to pass the torch onto you. He faced incredible sorrows and struggles, yet he did not allow them to knock him down. I have faced deep sorrows and struggles, yet I have not allowed them to pull my feet out to never walk again. You have faced or are facing unfair sorrows and struggles, and you, too, have everything within you to defeat opposition. Make room for that new hope to dance and sing again.

What difficulties, struggles, and hardships are you facing right now? Are you being pulled in multiple directions with smothering fear, loss, or change? Are you in a particular season with an increasing amount of worry and doubt? What struggle in your childhood has a foothold on you, keeping you from becoming an inspiration and hope to others who share the same struggles? What is your story?

I believe Abraham Lincoln put on the gloves of **FAITH, HOPE,** and **PERSEVERANCE**; he pressed on during his trials. He probably took two steps forward, then one step back; regardless, he didn't quit. Look at this remarkable man's character that came out of his hardships. We do not have to be a president with troubles and sorrows to achieve greatness.

"NO!" I proclaim with a stern but sincere and loving tone. This type of personal growth is not for just certain types of people, but it is for all who dare to wear those same gloves. Let your hands be surrounded by the gloves of faith, hope, and perseverance. Wear them until they get dirty and tattered with holes. Then, toss them in the trash can and get a new pair! Don't give up, because your gloves have holes in them!

In recent years, our family had a year with a collection of life changes and new seasons, which felt overwhelming and confusing at times. There were many wonderful blessings as a result of some intense growing pains. I'm sure glad I had those special gloves on to seek support and allow God to do a good work in me. Without change, we remain the same person, status quo.

\* \* \*

Close your eyes and imagine seeing the greatness developing within you by your *not* giving up. What non-material gem could possibly be waiting for you? What character refinement is going on inside of you as you turn the corner of that difficult road?

I would NEVER say that losing my dad or losing my sister Tammy made me a "better" or "greater" person. Some people carry around that philosophy. No, it's not like that. Have I learned so much about myself, my faith, and my ability to become stronger within? Yes. Have I learned to walk again with part of me missing from the hard losses? Yes. Have I learned that creating memories in the midst of uncomfortable change is worth far more than gold? Yes. Have I learned that resources and supportive people surround us, offering hope in any situation? Yes. Have I learned to sit at Jesus' feet daily and weep, that it will bring healing? Yes.

Working through my hard times is what took me onto a path where I could see the great transformation within me that was to be used in offering hope and inspiration to others. Even through the sorrow, the pain, and the tears - God says I am pretty great! He believed I had some hope-filled things to share with friends, family, and YOU.

\* \* \*

YOU are pretty great, too! Believe that you have a story to share from your pain and tough moments that will inspires others. It really happens. Hope. Hope follows the pain. If you won't grab the torch of hope from me or Abraham Lincoln, then get it from Jesus. He can be your guide and anchor in your hope-finding journey.

I am so glad we met through the pages of this book. I believe in you and would love to hear your story. You got this! Send me an email on how you are using your torch and what your *Hope Follows*.

* * *

### *Hope Follows YOUR hard story*

* * *

*"You are of God, little children, and have overcome them, because He who is in you is **greater** than he who is in the world." 1 John 4:4*

**Big Idea** - Two things you may want to do: tell a person in your life who has given you hope that they have encouraged you, and find someone you can encourage. How about we both pick up our phones and do it now. Ready, set, go!

# Acknowledgements

*"Piglet noticed that even though he had a very small heart, it could hold a rather large amount of gratitude."* A.A. Milne

\* \* \*

Drum roll please. This is the moment I have been waiting for. I'm a pretty small person, and I bet I might get smaller as I get older. I know it can happen, and I think it's just fine. If God wants us to get a little shorter in our more mature years, then that is just fine indeed. But, this little lady comes with a huge heart that overflows with gratitude. Picture it like a great surfing wave in Hawaii. The more I dwell on gratitude, the bigger it gets. Come join me as I tell you a little bit about some very special people who helped this book come to life.

\* \* \*

To Kurt, my husband of 28 years and counting, I can still vividly remember the day we sat at my favorite resort for dinner in December 2013. It had been about six weeks after losing

Tammy, and you gave me the most beautiful, thoughtful gift. The bracelet with the poem made me cry so hard. Your intricate details in the writing and the design and stone color on the bracelet were so eloquently chosen as a significant reminder of my relationship with Tam. You were my biggest support and took on many duties around the house early in my grief recovery. Plus, all the extra help this past year with my tons of 12 hour writing sessions do not go unnoticed! Thank you for feeding me when I wouldn't move from my desk, as I cried out, "I am not doing anything for anyone today!" You know all the trips I took back to Indiana and Chicago? Those were so vital to my healing of grief, and you didn't blink an eye when I wanted to go again. Thank you, Kurt, for all the free tickets you let me use from the Southwest Airlines Visa miles. Mostly, your unending strength and selfless emotional support are solid guardrails that kept me on the path. Let's celebrate this 20 year book dream being fulfilled! Muchas gracias, my forever love!

\* \* \*

Dearest Karen, Alex, and Maggie, how I couldn't have been more thrilled to have you as my outstanding editors. I am in tears right now writing this little note of thanks. Thank you! Thank you! Thank you! The time, heart, and effort you put into fine tuning my writing meant the world to me. I depended on the ideas you offered and corrections you suggested. That work, ladies, became such a vital part in the completion of this book project. I laughed at some of the errors you found, thinking to myself out loud, "What in the world was I thinking there?!" We did it, ladies!!! I love you all! And just a few words to each of you....

Karen, my beautiful and creative sister-in-law, I love having you in my life and the joy and wisdom you give so freely. With you, there is never a boring moment; you bring so much fun and color to our world. We need a sister visit to play some *Yahtzee*, because your brother won't play with me.

Alex, my lovely and elegant daughter-in-law, from the day I first met you by the high school fountain, as a new friend of Jack's, I knew there was something very special about you. Now, you are a Kenzler! Praise God! You are wise, resourceful and such an incredible wife to Jack. Our family is so much more with you in it.

Maggie, my precious and beautiful daughter, how I love watching your heart for foster children and seniors continues to grow. Here you are, a co-editor, of my book, and it seems only yesterday you were waltzing around the house with your pink "click clack" dress-up shoes. I cannot even count how many times you asked me how I was doing in the early years after losing Aunt Tam; that meant so much to me, Maggie. Thank you for your tender, compassionate heart and big hugs. They were my lifeline at times when I was limp with sadness.

\* \* \*

To Jack, my first born child, thank you for rocking the cover design! The leaves have so much meaning, and you know what speaks to my heart. Thank you for your talent; I'm in awe at the creative design work you do. Aren't you glad we did lots of arts and crafts when you were younger?! How crazy to think you were a young boy running around the house when I first talked about my ideas for writing a book. Now, you are my designer! How can I express my thankfulness for your care and love during that first year after losing Aunt Tammy? You were a high school senior and could have been hanging out with your friends after your half days; but no, you checked on me. At times, I was afraid to be home alone, fearing that I would hyperventilate from too much crying. Thank you for being there for me. I love you, Jackie!

To Ryan, my second son, thank you for being my biggest promoter on social media! When I saw your posts about a "project Lady Jewels has in the works," I was stunned at the reality that I better get it done! I thought out loud, "Ryan just shared about it, so he must believe in me!" Thank you for your support and input with Jack's design work. You guys make a dynamic team! I remember driving you home from swim practice one day after losing Aunt Tam, when I completely lost my composure and began shaking and sobbing. I cried so hard, and you let me hold your hand really tight. The feeling I had was similar to a young child walking along a very scary bridge and needing to hold someone's hand. You helped me to be brave that day. Thank you and I love you, Ry Ry!

To Evan, my baby of the family, thank you for picking up all the things I left lying around the house during the writing phase of this book. You encouraged me, served me food, took care of the dogs, got me water, gave a quick shoulder massage and anything else I needed. I am sorry you were so young when we lost Aunt Tam, and you didn't have as many memories as your siblings. Nonetheless, she loved all her many nieces and nephews with all her heart. You kiddos were her abundant joy. When the going got rough in the onset of the 2020 Covid-19 Pandemic, I continued to hold onto our special Tuesdays and Thursdays, Evan. Remember, you were the one who noticed my renewed joyfulness after so much grief work? You are wise beyond your years, and your gentle strength will be to your advantage in the career path you choose. I can't wait to see the opportunities God opens up for you. I love you, Evie!

\* \* \*

To my dear friends, Gloria and Tonya, who encouraged me and believed in me as a writer and published author. The example you set for taking your own dreams to completion fueled my passion and drive to get this project done. Gloria, you also experienced tragedy and how incredible the way God is using you to minister to women who need that hope. I can't wait to work on a book project together! Tonya, you held my hand as I fell apart after hearing the "not guilty" verdict of the drunk driver, though we all knew he was guilty. Thank you for being there and making Evan dinner that night. I think we need to go back to the spa where we first made our commitments to chase our dreams. It's time to celebrate and relax! You said you wanted to start a business and did accomplish that. I said I would write a book, and I just did it. Now, the time it took doesn't even matter; it's completed! Thanks for not giving up on me. You ladies are both so talented in your fields, and I am blessed to call you friends. I love you, Gloria and Tonya!

Here's a big shout out to all my family and friends who have been reading my blog stories over the years and encouraging me to put my voice and words into a book. Every comment on a blog post or email built up my confidence in becoming a published author. Thank you a million times over for your part in *Hope Follows*.

To my new friends reading this book and meeting me for the

first time, thank you for coming along on this journey with *Hope Follows*. I pray you have discovered that you can *reclaim hope and joy* in the aftermath of your life's battles and struggles. May you also experience the kind of bold, restorative hope that God offers through Jesus Christ. It'll be the ride of your life.

To Dawn, my grief counselor, thank you for all our talks, your prayers, and the counsel you provided for me in a very fragile time in my life. I recall the first day I stepped into your office, and I just collapsed in tears. You listened with the most compassionate and wise heart. The best advice I received from you: "For this you have Jesus, Julie" Yes, so true. I wonder if you still have the glass I made you with those words painted on it in puffy paint!

\* \* \*

Most important of all to Almighty God ~ forever, I am grateful to you, for holding me and comforting me during the tragic grief. You are my source for the ideas, insights, and inspiration in this book. I could be driving my car, shopping for groceries, or hiking with my dogs, and SNAP, just like that a story or object lesson pops into my head. Quickly, I grab a notepad from my purse or open up my phone's voice recorder app to narrate and take notes. Thanks for making me feel like a top news reporter. Remember, how I loved writing news stories in sixth grade and in high school, God? Of course, you do. Your vast, awesome ways never cease to amaze me. Thank you for putting my talents into a work that can build up your kingdom. You are my all in all.

# Epilogue

My prayer for you ~

*Dear Lord, help my friend to live one day at a time so they may meet each day's challenge with grace, courage, and hope. Keep them from the fears of the future and the anguish of the past. Help their mind and heart to stay focused on the present, where the true gift of happiness and healing are found.*

*In Jesus' name, Amen.*

\* \* \*

*Because of you in my life, Tammy, I have been changed for good.*

# Author Information

\* \* \*

Has your *HOPE FOLLOWS* story started?
What is it like? Have you shared it with anyone?
I would love to hear **your** story!
Email: juliekenzler@gmail.com
Facebook: *Hope Follows*
Instagram: *hope_follows*
Blog Website: www.hopefollows.com

\* \* \*

# *Notes*

NAVIGATING THE WAVES

1    Grief Share grief recovery support group. https://www.griefshare.org/

A DISTRACTED MOUSE

2    Northshore University Health System. "Take it Easy: The Benefits of Relaxation." December 18, 2018.